STAGE & CRAFT

Roy A. Beck

Western Michigan University

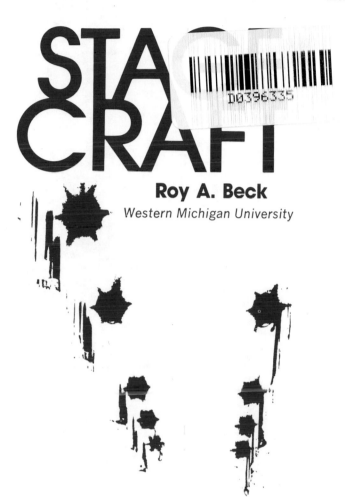

NTC *NATIONAL TEXTBOOK COMPANY* • *Lincolnwood, Illinois U.S.A.*

To my father, Rudy Beck, who was always building something for someone; from whom I learned the meaning of craftsmanship.

Introduction

In play production, stagecraft is just one part of the total process. Stagecraft is planning, building, and coordinating scenery, lights, props, and sound to resemble the setting the playwright describes. The crafts, which are vital and necessary to give the audience the scenic effect, are known as *stagecraft*.

We are all builders of some kind. Producing a play requires several kinds of building. Acting requires building a character aside from your own personality. The various crafts of technical theatre are likewise methods of building. Scene design consists of building mental images for the set in which the actor builds his characterization. Scene construction, lights, props, and sound continue to build and complete the mental images of the playwright, designer, and director. When you are involved in play production there is another kind of building, the building within yourself. More than just carpentry, electrical, or sound engineering skills, you are learning about yourself. You learn the skills, the limits of those skills, their potential development, and how your confidence increases as you use them.

The arts of the theatre are practical arts in that you must experience them. You must DO them to know them. No textbook can "give" you the experience you will get when you build your first flat, make your first prop, or "run" lights or sound.

Stagecraft is a how-to-do volume—how to design, how to construct, light, prop, and sound a show. The methods described are by no means the only way the crafts can be applied. Both standard and innovative, they are methods I have learned, created, used, and taught to my students. They worked for those who taught me, they have worked for me, and they can work for you. By using different methods you may produce the same effect, or you may produce a new and different effect. As you learn you can adapt to achieve a desired effect. It is essential, however, that you know the *basic method* before adapting it. I have attempted to present here some of the *basic methods*.

It is not possible to acknowledge all of the students who have helped build my sets in the past 25 years; not that I could recall all of them, but they will recognize their contribution to this volume. I thank them for then . . . and thank them for now.

For those in theatre, there is a thrill every time the curtain goes up or comes down for the final curtain call. I still get excited with the student at the personal thrill he experiences whether he has painted the throne on which *King Lear* sits, or if he is playing Lear. I hope you will experience that thrill and pride when you say, "I did that."

Roy A. Beck

Use of the masculine gender in this volume should not be considered as sexist; it is merely the way I learned to use the English language. Some of the finest and best technicians and crew members I have had have been female.

R. A. B.

Stagecraft

For many dramatics students producing a play means *acting* in a play. In the *total* process of play production, however, acting happens to be just *one* part. A much larger "cast" is required off-stage to effectively put on a play; scenery, lighting, sound effects, props, costumes, and make-up crews are *just as important* as acting in the play.

School plays or class plays should be just that—school or class ventures, meaning that everyone connected with the class should share in the enjoyment, thrill, and work of producing the play. The cooperation of many people make producing the play is a highlight of the school year. It requires the talents of any interested students who can offer help in the shop or with the art work, according to their special abilities. The personal success of finding a place where one is accepted for creative ability rather than for social or economic status is one of the biggest rewards of working behind the scenes. Ideally you should, if you are interested in theatre, work in as many areas of play production as is possible during your high school years. Developing your several talents in the theatre should be your personal goal.

THE STAGE

The stage is any space where the action of a play can take place. It is not necessarily the raised platform at the end or the side of the gym. Stages, like people, come in all sizes and shapes.

The *traditional stage* is divided into three basic parts (see Figure 1): the acting area, the apron, and the backstage area, which includes the wings to the right and left of the acting area. Usually these areas are enclosed in a frame called the proscenium arch, which frames the action of the play as a picture frame frames a picture. Many high schools in this country have limited their play productions to the picture-frame concept; that is, all of the action of the play takes place in the confines of the proscenium arch. In recent years, forward-thinking designers and directors in the theatre have tried to overcome this tendency by developing new concepts of staging. Arena staging and thrust or open staging are two examples of these new types.

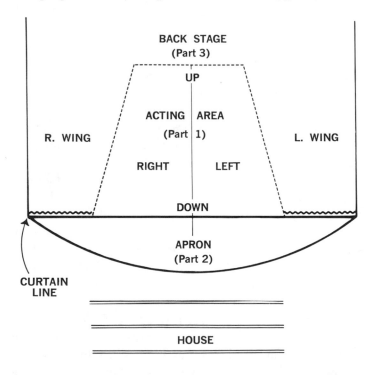

Fig. 1. The Traditional Stage.

Arena staging was one of the first new concepts. In this type of staging the actors occupy a center area, called the central acting area, and the audience is seated very close to the actors on all four sides of the arena (see Figure 2). Some directors refer to arena staging as "acting in the round," for the audience surrounds the actors. Professor Glenn Hughes in his book, *Penthouse Theatre,* illustrates how arena staging can be accomplished in varied situations. Flexibility is the prime advantage of arena staging; practically any interior setting can be staged arena style, or a modification of it. One variation of the arena type seats the audience on three sides of the acting area and uses the fourth side for the setting and large pieces of scenery. The author staged Noel Coward's *Blithe Spirit* in a church assembly hall, using three sides for the audience and a natural wall of french doors for the setting and for Elvira's entrance.

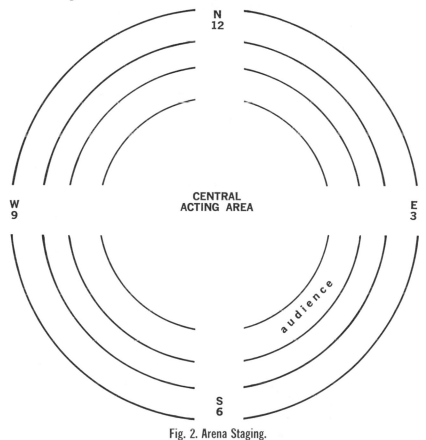

Fig. 2. Arena Staging.

Audiences in arena staging normally are kept small, i.e., 100 to 200 for each performance. The small audience offers a real advantage for budding thespians; it means more performances. Settings in the "round" should be kept to a minimum—usually just large props, such as tables, chairs, benches, etc. Care should be taken not to block the audience's view with tall scenery. It is typical that most plays currently produced in high schools have interior settings. Such settings offer unlimited possibilities for arena staging. Nearly every school has an area that can be used for an arena stage: the cafeteria, study hall, large lobby, choral room, or perhaps the gym floor can be converted to an intimate arena stage with only a little creative imagination and work.

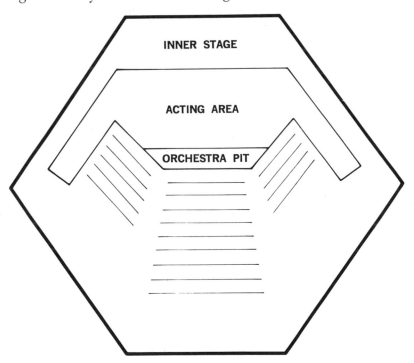

INNER STAGE

ACTING AREA

ORCHESTRA PIT

Fig. 3. Thrust stage.

The most recent development in staging is the *open* or *thrust stage* (see Figure 3). Mr. James Hull Miller is credited with developing this concept in his design of the Western Springs Theatre at Western Springs, Illinois. In effect, the apron of the traditional stage is extended into the house. The audience is seated on three sides of the "thrust" stage and the acting area is moved forward so that most of the play's action takes place "down front." Settings usually are placed to the rear of the thrust and some directors have effectively employed "projected" scenery by using a slide projector and painting the set design on the slides. Modifications of the thrust stage can be used in any high school by building a stage extension of fifteen or twenty feet onto the apron.

High school play directors have always been called upon to be creative and innovative in staging plays. Plays have been produced in large classrooms and lunch rooms, and the author recalls a high school group that converted an old coal bin (the school had converted to gas heat) into a wonderful little theatre seating about 150 people. Where in your school could a play be produced other than the auditorium?

The purpose of the stage can be stated simply: "To put life into action where all (the audience) can see it."

In the drawing of the stage acting area in Figure 1 all directions are given in terms of the actor as he faces the audience. "Up" is *away* from the audience; "down" is *toward* the audience. At one point in theatre history the stage was built as an inclined plane sloping toward the audience, which was seated on a flat floor. Thus a move "up" meant a move up the incline and "down" meant to move down the incline. The great operatic composer, Richard Wagner, was one of the first to raise the audience on a sloped floor and to level out the stage. The terms "up" and "down," however, have remained a part of stage terminology.

Directions for arena stages (Figure 2) are given in one of two ways: (1) according to the points of the compass or (2) according to the hands of the clock. Acting in and directing for arena stages calls for a great deal of adaptation on the part of both actors and directors and, the author has found that the hands of the clock are a little more precise in directing movements and placing settings in arena stages. For the open or thrust stage, directions are given the same way as for the traditional stage.

SCENERY

Scenery is the environment or the locale of the play, created on the stage. As an environment, scenery should suggest to the audience where and when the play is taking place. Location (where) and time (when) are the two basic purposes for scenery on any stage or screen. How these two elements are achieved is determined by the stage, the equipment, and the talents of the scenic artist. (See Fig. 4.)

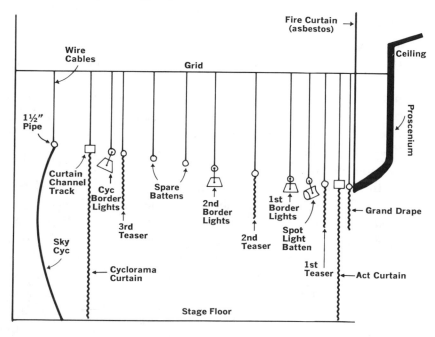

Fig. 4. Cross-Section of a Traditional Stage.

Scenery may be simple, or highly complex, and still achieve the two basic purposes of location and time. In your high school the stage might serve as a wrestling practice area, student council meeting room, cheerleader practice area, band practice area, and for countless other functions in addition to the speech and drama function for which it was intended. If scheduling the stage is a problem in your school, the author advises keeping scenery simple! Overly ambitious and elaborate stage scenery, without adequate time or equipment to do a good job of it, is one of the biggest problems in high school theatre. Good scenery should contribute to the *total* presentation of the play. It should not stand out or detract from the total production; and if it is badly done, it will! Before you attempt to design and make scenery for your play it is necessary to know about methods of staging.

Fig. 5. Stylized setting for "Oedipus Rex," Western Michigan University, Laura V. Shaw Theatre. Directed by Zack York, designed by Vern Stillwell.

METHODS OF STAGING

The action of most plays takes place either inside or outside; inside action is called "interior" and outside action is called "exterior" action. Occasionally, plays have no specific setting, and such settings are called "formal" or "space" settings. Many classical Greek plays are staged in this fashion, as well as most Shakespearean plays. Locale and time in formal settings are usually indicated by costumes, program notation, and the language of the actors.

A bare stage with dramatic downshafts of light can be used for some types of plays, usually those not realistic in nature. Fantasies, dream plays, and psychodramas—in addition to the classical and Shakespearean plays—can be staged on a bare stage using minimum lighting and curtains.

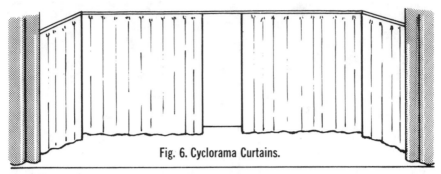

Fig. 6. Cyclorama Curtains.

Nearly every high school is equipped with a set of cyclorama curtains: i.e., the curtains on the inside of the proscenium arch surround the acting area. (Cyclorama means "surrounding," referred to as a "cyc" by most people in the theatre.) Cyc settings have been used very effectively for many high school plays, and it is one of the easiest and simplest settings. By the addition of selected properties, the cyc setting can resemble nearly any locale. Add a couch and chairs and the scene becomes a living room (many plays take place in living rooms); add a table and chairs and the scene becomes a kitchen or dining room (depending upon the style of the table and chairs). The element of historical time can be indicated by costumes. The properties selected for the cyc setting should fit the style of the play and also may indicate time. It is possible to add doors and windows to the cyc set when they are needed. The cyc curtains can be parted and the door or window frame inserted into the cyc. The cyc curtains may be artistically draped back, or, if the cyc has built-in headers (short pieces of curtain that make a natural door opening [see Figure 7]),the door or window unit can be inserted here.

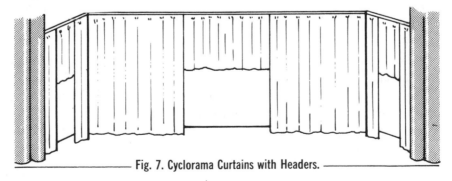

Fig. 7. Cyclorama Curtains with Headers.

Exterior settings occasionally are needed, and they too can be placed in a cyc setting (see Figure 8). Simple trees and "ground row" low foliage, plants, and flowers can be painted on Upson board (available from most lumber yards in 4' x 8' sheets) and cut out with a coping saw or trim knife. A cyc set can be used for plays which have more than one setting. Rapid changes can be made with cyc settings, and they are quite effective when properly used.

Fig. 8. Exterior set pieces.

SET PIECES

A modification of the cyc setting is the "set piece" setting. Set pieces are key or important pieces of scenery that are required by the plot of the play. In the two-act drama, *The Staring Match,* by Jerry McNeely, it is necessary to have an old-fashioned well on the stage for the opening and the closing scenes. The well, constructed of 1" x 3" and Upson board, is placed on the stage for the opening scene, removed for most of the play, and returned for the final scene. This is a "set piece." Without it the plot of the play is not complete.

The popular high school drama *The Curious Savage* requires a set of french doors and bookcases located up center. These pieces, plus entrances, are all that are really required, yet the stage is commonly filled with scenery for this play. Creative use of the imagination can simplify the task of the stage setting and save the stage crew precious time and class treasury money.

Fig. 9. Western Michigan University's production of "West Side Story," presented in the James W. Miller Auditorium   Directed by Robert L. Smith, designed by Roy Beck.

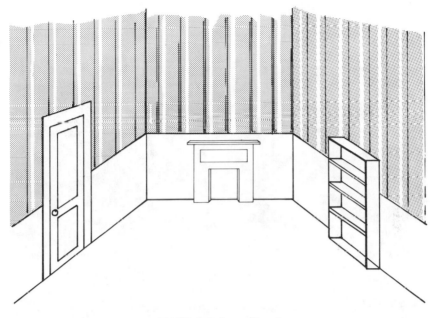

Fig. 10. Interior profile set.

PROFILE SETS

An extension of the set piece setting is the "profile set." Profiles (see Figure 10) are "suggested" full sets, but are seldom full height. Walls are suggested by laying flats on the long side rather than standing them upright, which makes a wall about five feet high. Doors and window units are placed, but there is no attempt to hide entrances or exits of actors (unless required by the plot) by surrounding them with flats or cyc curtains. Settings in profile can be as realistically or suggestively done as the director wishes. The author has, on occasion, merely suggested a door opening with upright pieces of 1" x 6", and walls with pieces of Upson board stapled to a 1" x 2" frame, cut in an irregular shape to avoid too many parallel lines. Profiles should be high enough to be seen and recognized by the audience. A variety of heights adds visual interest. You can create many interesting and exciting effects with profile sets.

FULL SET

Fig. 11. Full realistic setting for Western Michigan University production "Look Back in Anger," (Laura V. Shaw Theatre), directed by Robert L. Smith, designed by Roy Beck.

A full set consists of stage scenery (flats) from the curtain line stage right to the curtain line stage left with little or no interruption. There are many variations and degrees of full settings. The typical full set is the "box set." With a box set you attempt to enclose the acting area with a realistic room set, and all three walls are created with flats. In most schools the box set will be the first thing considered, after the play is selected. Under four conditions, a full setting should be used: (1) there must be adequate time to design and build the set; (2) there must be adequate space for building and/or painting scenery; (3) proper tools and equipment must be available; and (4) no other method of staging can be used effectively.

Regardless of the method of staging, it must be remembered that the available facilities, your talent as a scenic artist, and the time allotted for scenery construction determine the quality of the set for the play. Of these limiting conditions, time is most important. A good play setting cannot be produced in the three days before the play is to be presented, or even a week before. When rehearsals begin for the play, work should begin on the set.

DESIGNING SCENERY

The first step in planning scenery, after you have selected the method of staging that fits your play, is designing the set. For many years high school plays have been produced with poorly copied sets from the pictures and floor plans in the back of the play script. The sets pictured in the play script are usually from a Broadway production where cost was not an important factor, and they were designed for a stage far better equipped than most high school stages. Your high school stage is not the stage of the Helen Hayes Theatre—why copy a set designed for it? The obvious disadvantages are too much scenery for a small stage, far too elaborate set decoration, and construction that can be done only by professional designers and carpenters. A final disadvantage is the lack of creativity. The hurried, harassed, overworked play director, who does not have time properly to create the scenery, should utilize the talents of his students in this area of design. Much has been written about the esthetic qualities of scenery design (see the bibliography) which is of much greater scope than one could hope to give in an entire book the size of this one. What is intended here is a *practical* approach to designing scenery.

Step 1. Read the play at least twice before attempting to design anything. A designer needs to be familiar with all aspects of the play. Nearly all plays require certain things, as prescribed by the playwright, i.e., doors, windows, levels, special pieces of furniture or fixtures. During the second reading, make a list of what is *required* by the play. Note the locations suggested by the script and other possible locations that might be used.

Step 2. Confer with the director. Secure his ideas and suggestions concerning the set design. Every director has in his mind's eye a picture of what he believes the finished play set should look like. His reasons for selecting the play sometimes are based upon the ease of set construction. Most director's theatrical experiences can be of invaluable aid to a designer. Make careful written notes of his suggestions.

Step 3. Research the historical period of the play. This activity is particularly useful for period plays, and is very helpful for some early 20th century plays. A play always takes place at a given time and that specific time must be projected visually to the audience. With these preliminary data, the designer is ready to approach the stage on which the play set is to be built.

Step 4. How much space is available? Equipped with ruler, yardstick, or a 25-foot tape ruler, the designer takes the measurements. How much room does the set require? How much backstage room is there for bracing, passage for actors, prop storage, etc.? How much room do the actors need on stage? Will the proposed set aid the actor rather than hinder him? These questions can be answered only by knowing the amount of space on the stage. Measure the stage from the act curtain to the back wall and from the edge of the act curtain right to the edge of the act curtain left, when the curtain is fully open. Then measure from the cyc curtain up right to the cyc curtain up left.

Step 5. Determine the sightlines for your stage. Sit in the front of the auditorium as far right as possible; then look at the stage. How much of the offstage area can you see? Look both right and left and especially note how much of the backstage area is exposed near the front curtain line. Next, move to the far left of the auditorium and repeat the procedure. If your stage is in the gym, you will need to set up a chair where the front row is usually placed for play performances. It might be wise to check with the head custodian since he usually is in charge of setting up the chairs. If your auditorium has a balcony, it must be checked as well, particularly from the front-row seat in the center, as you observe the approximate set height. Sightlines help you determine how much the act curtain must be closed after the set is constructed to hide or mask, the backstage area. You may want to experiment with the sightlines by closing the curtain just a little and taking another look at the stage. Be sure to measure how far the curtain is closed.

Step 6. Make a floor plan of the set. With the dimensions you have from your measurement of the stage and the sightlines, be-

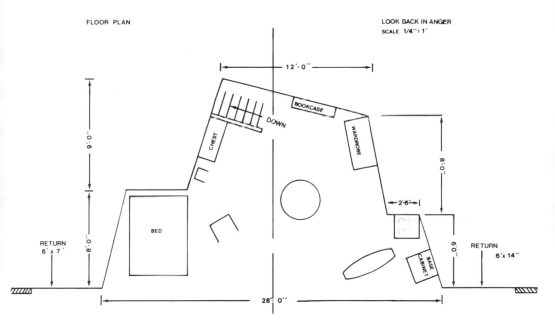

FLOOR PLAN

LOOK BACK IN ANGER
SCALE 1/4″: 1′

Fig. 12. "Look Back in Anger" floor plan.

gin a rough floor plan of the set. First draw a scale diagram of
the stage (½″ equaling 1′ is excellent for this purpose). Now
plan the placement of major set props, furniture, etc., taking note
of the director's suggestions and ideas concerning how much acting space is needed. First, place the doors and windows (if the
set calls for them); next, place the necessary platforms; and lastly,
locate the flats that make up the background. The size of each
flat should be indicated on the floor plan so you know exactly
how much room the total set will take on the stage.

Step 7. Make a rough perspective sketch of the set. A rough
sketch of the set is not difficult to execute; you do not have to be
an artist to make this working sketch. Begin with a line indicating
the center of the stage and construct a box around the center line
representing the stage house. On the back and sides of the box
you can detail parts of the set. If you encounter difficulty, ask the

art teacher for help. Be sure you indicate colors on the rough perspective with colored pencil, crayon, or water colors.

Step 8. Make a model of the set. Making a set model is an activity that many students enjoy. Using the floor plan and the

LOOK BACK IN ANGER   Description of Flats:

Stage Right	Size	Special	Paint
1. Return	6′ x 7′		black, gray base,
2. R-1	4′ x 7′	casement window	etc.
3. R-2	4′ x 7′	2′ x 2′,	
4. R-3	5′ x 7′	4″ up/bottom	
5. R-4	4′6″ x 7′		
6. R-5	4′6″ x 7′		
7. R-6	6′ x 7′		

Stage Left			
1. Return	6′ x 14′		black,
2. L-1	6′ x 14′		gray base,
3. L-2	2′6″ x 14′		spatter dk. brown,
4. L-3	4′ x 14′		olive, black
5. L-4	4′ x 14′		
6. L-5	6′ x 7′		

Special
SR-1   triangle 3′ x 6′ (fits atop R-6)
SL-2   3′ and 7′ stiles x 6′ bottom rail
             (fits atop L-5)

SL-2 has casement type windows 1′ up from bottom rail and is full 6′ wide 2′ high.

SET WILL SPLIT AT L-5 and R-6. Left side to be stored behind blacks at the rear left. Right side to be stored behind blacks at the rear right.

Fig. 13. Flat list for "Look Back in Anger."

rough sketch you have made, begin your model set by making flats of heavy cardboard, using the ½″ equals 1′ scale. Make each flat individually, just as you plan to do it on the stage. Lightweight cardboard or illustration board is excellent for this purpose. Once you have cut out with a razor blade or knife the flats to be used, paint them (with water colors or tempera) the color you and the director have selected for the set. (This is a good time to experiment with various colors.) The model should be decorated the way you intend to decorate the finished set. Plastic doll furniture can be used to furnish the set, but it is possible to make the furniture from cardboard or balsa wood. During the model construction you will encounter problems much like those in building the real set.

It should be noted that not all designers follow all of the steps outlined here. Many excellent professional designers have never worked from a model; others have never made a rough perspective. If you are seriously interested in scene design, further study of books on scene design and as much practice as you can get is recommended.

Figure 13 is a description of the flats selected from permanent stock and units to be constructed (under "Special") for *Look Back in Anger*. Once the design has been approved by the director, the flats and scenery units to make the setting need to be selected. Full set walls can be put together in a number of different ways using various sizes of flats. Stability and ease of handling, particularly if there are scene shifts involved, should determine which flats are selected to make up the set walls. Trying various combinations on the stage can sometimes aid in the selection. Once the flats are selected each should be numbered L for left and R for right, with notes on the individual flat repairs, color and special treatment. Such a chart is of great value to the stage crew in getting the set ready and up for the show.

ARENA SCENERY

Plays staged in arena style normally do not require scenery as extensive as that used on the traditional stage. When plays are produced in the full round, they usually require only furniture or property setting. When a modified arena is used, either three-sided or half round, low pieces of scenery can be used. Screen settings (see page 20) in arena staging should be used because the audience usually is very close to the play's action. If the audience is close, a good deal of attention should be given to construction detail to ensure well-made sets.

The designing of sets for the arena follows the same basic steps outlined for the traditional stage, but the designer should note that what is acceptable for an audience in proscenium staging may not be acceptable in arena. Extreme artificiality, unless it is a part of the play, will not be accepted by most audiences because they are so much a part of the play. Designs for arena settings

Fig. 14. Composite set for the production of "Purlie Victorious" by Western Michigan's Arena Theatre, directed by Robert L. Smith.

should consider: (1) the minimum essential set pieces, (2) entrance and exit of actors, and (3) utilization of the playing space.

Composite settings in arena designs fuse all parts or places into a single set within the playing space. Certain areas of the space can be designated as the living room, dining room, and courtyard. These areas usually overlap in the center of the playing space. *Single sets,* as in the traditional stage, represent a specific locale, usually a room, and the decoration must convey to the audience the element of time. The placement of furniture is very important since it should not block the action of the play and the action should be visible to most of the audience.

In any form of arena staging it is imperative that the director and the designer work together.

MAKING SCENERY

Two people in most schools can help the stage crew beyond measure in building scenery: the school custodian and the industrial arts teacher. Both of these men have many duties to perform, and it is a *wise* stage crew that tactfully approaches both men early in the stages of play production and asks for their assistance.

If the school does not have a scene shop as a part of its stage facilities, the next area of the school properly equipped for mak ing scenery is the industrial arts department. Making scenery calls for precision cutting of materials, and this can best be accomplished with power equipment. If tactfully approached, most industrial arts teachers are willing to help stage crews cut out, and in some cases assemble, scenery. This does not mean that the responsibility for building the scenery is given to the industrial arts teacher; building scenery is the responsibility of the scenery crew. Should members of the stage crew know how to handle power equipment (such knowledge usually comes from an industrial arts course in woodworking), the request may be to use the school's equipment in building the scenery. If your school is fortunate enough to have a scene shop with power equipment, it is important that only members of the crew who know how to handle power equipment do so. Power saws, particularly, are dangerous in the hands of people who do not know how to use them.

School custodians are familiar with the places stage crews can find the things—in and out of the school—that are needed to build scenery, and local sources of supply are valuable to any stage crew. Using the stage for scenery building also presents problems for the custodian, unless he is consulted before the crew begins work. Custodians are among the most valuable "friends" any play-producing group can have. Needless to say, both individuals should be given program credit for their help in producing the play. Having consulted both the industrial arts teacher and the custodian, the scenery crew is ready to go to work.

Basic Flat and Screen Construction. A "flat" consists of a wooden frame covered with muslin or canvas; it is usually from 10′ to 16′ in height. A "screen" differs only in height; it is from 6′ to 9′ high. Stage scenery, in general, is not constructed with permanence in mind, although flats and screens usually last from three to five years, or even longer, depending upon care and use. Scenery is not built "solid as a rock," as one would build a home or a shop project. Scenery should be lightweight, easily moved, and adaptable to a variety of situations. A flat resembles an artist's canvas; indeed, the historical origin of flats was in renaissance Italy, where some of the great artists were employed for scenic painting.

Standard Size Flats

Width	Recommended Height
5′ 9″	10′ – 12′
4′ 0″	10′ – 12′
3′ 6″	10′ – 12′
3′ 0″	10′ – 12′
2′ 6″	10′ – 12′
2′ 0″	10′– 12′
1′ 0″	10′ – 12′

Flat sizes, and particularly their height, depend upon the height of the proscenium opening and whether or not the curtain borders are adjustable up and down. Very tall flats on a small stage tend to give the illusion of a very high ceilinged room. Further, they tend to give an air of formality to whatever play is done. In most school situations, 10′ to 12′ flats give a much more intimate feeling, a desirable characteristic for most modern plays. Flat widths are more historical than practical. Flats were made 5′ to 9′ wide simply because that was the size of the door opening on old railway cars and also the size of the stage door. Practically speaking, a flat can be *any* width, according to its purpose. What the author listed above is a so-called "stock" set of flats, usable for many plays and stage purposes. If your school does not have a set of flats it is best to begin with the stock sizes listed above. Since flats will need to be used from play to play and year to year, it is important that they be a *standard* size. Flats wider than 5′ 9″ are difficult to handle and to store on the stage.

Recommended Screen Sizes

Width	Height
5′ 0″	8′ – 9′
4′ 0″	8′ – 9′
3′ 0″	8′ – 9′
2′ 0″	8′ – 9′
1′ 0″	8′ – 9′

Screens are recommended for schools with minimum stage facilities and a small stage area. Screens have the advantage over regular flats in that they are lighter in weight and more easily moved. Screens work better as set pieces and in profile sets than do regular flats. Most plays produced in high schools do not require extreme "realistic" or "naturalistic" settings but rather require only an illusion on the stage. Screens fulfill this requirement very effectively.

In making a flat or screen: (1) select the lumber; (2) cut the lumber; (3) assemble the flat or screen; and (4) cover the flat or screen.

Selecting lumber for the construction of flats or screens is an important task. The first decision is whether the flat or screen is to be used only for one play, or added to the permanent stock of scenery. Permanent flats are usually constructed with better grades of lumber than temporary scenery. Temporary, or one-show flats can be made from several common grades of lumber. Firring strips (1" x 2"), used in the home to panel walls, can be used as well as common grades of 1" x 3" and 1" x 4". Lumber is classified today as "common" and "Upper." Upper is better than common. Within each classification are several grades; upper grades are "B and Better," C, and D; common grades are 2, 3, and 4. Nationally, the dimensions of lumber have changed in order to conserve lumber which is growing short in supply. What is called 1" x 3" in this text, and by most lumberyards, has actual dimensions of $\frac{3}{4}$" x $2\frac{1}{2}$"; a 2" x 4" actually measures $1\frac{1}{2}$" x $3\frac{1}{2}$". Lumbermen still use the *full inch* dimensions when referring to lumber stock. Flats to be added to the permanent stock of scenery should be constructed from the upper grades of lumber which are generally clearer, have fewer knots and less warp. A permanent flat, properly constructed, can serve for years and be remodeled several times for other plays. White pine is preferred to other woods because of its durability, close grain, and ease of working. If white pine is not available, or the cost is prohibitive in your area, fir is the next best choice. Two by fours are generally available in fir rather than pine. Fir does have a tendency to split and splinter rather easily.

Learning to select lumber is an experience stage crew members should have, and for this reason it is strongly recommended that they personally visit the lumber company to help select the lumber for the play. The personnel of most lumber yards have a great deal of knowledge about wood and its use that is invaluable to a stage crew member. Lumber should be inspected to make certain all pieces will meet the needs of the set to be built—even the "common" grades vary considerably in knots and warp. Selec-

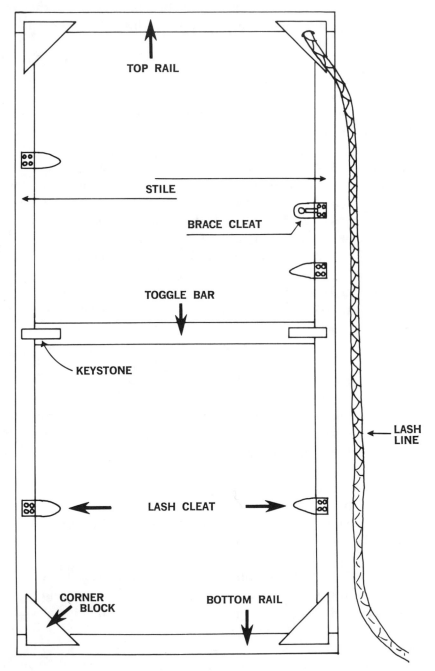

TOP RAIL

STILE

BRACE CLEAT

TOGGLE BAR

KEYSTONE

LASH
LINE

LASH CLEAT

CORNER
BLOCK

BOTTOM RAIL

Fig. 15. Parts of a flat,

tion should be made to get stock as straight as possible. Knots can frequently be worked around in the cutting process. If lumber is ordered by phone, the grade, thickness, width (in full inches) and length should be stated. It is also wise to inquire about the cost, since lumber prices are usually on the increase. Waste should be kept to a bare minimum, but crews and directors are apt to make mistakes in figuring, cutting or laying out the scenery. Therefore, it is wise to order more than is absolutely essential to build the necessary units. Ordering stock in longer lengths (12' and 16') assures a sufficient supply of lumber on hand when needed. Lumber companies figure lumber in *board feet*, whereas most flats are figured in *lineal feet* (and soon meters). To avoid the board feet lineal feet confusion it is best to order lumber by the number of lengths (12' or 16') needed. For example: a single 5' x 10' flat requires four (4) 12' lengths, with about 4'-6" left over for a toggle bar on another flat.

Cutting the Lumber: Figure 15 represents the parts of a flat. The top and bottom are called *rails;* the side pieces are called *stiles;* the center brace is called a *toggle bar.* Each flat or screen consists of five pieces:

2 rails—cut the exact width of the finished flat or screen.

2 stiles—cut 2 times the width of the stock *less* than the finished height of the flat or screen.

1 toggle bar—cut 2 times the width of the stock *less* than the finished width of the flat.

A square should be used to mark all cuts, even when using power saws with cross-cut gauges and guides. Before making any cuts it is wise to check and *double check* all measurements. Always allow one-sixteenth inch for saw cuts. Once the rails, stiles, and toggle bar have been cut, the assembly involves the following steps: (1) squaring the corners, (2) attaching the corner blocks, and (3) attaching the keystones.

Squaring the corners was, for a number of years, one of the major problems high school scenery crews had in making flats. Today, thanks to a picture-frame miter clamp, *any* scenery crew can build square flats. Picture-frame miter clamps can be purchased at nearly all hardware stores for a reasonable price. Make certain the clamps will open to 3", as they come in various

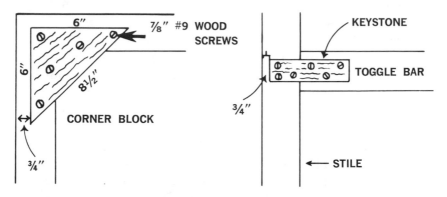

Fig. 16. Cornerblock and Keystone.

sizes. A scenery crew hard-pressed for cash can operate with one set, although two sets are recommended for assembly-line building. The picture-frame miter clamps are attached to the top rail and stiles by sliding the 1" x 3" into the clamp opening and screwing it tight. Make certain the rail and stile touch at each corner. Frequently, saw cuts will be uneven; so let the clamp square the corner! Do not force two unevenly cut pieces of wood together. The clamps should not be removed until the corner blocks have been attached.

Corner blocks are made from ¼" plywood cut in an 8½" x 6" triangle (see Figure 16). The grain on the top layer of plywood should run as is illustrated for maximum support. If the grain runs counter to this there is danger that the block will crack, as the top layers of plywood are stronger than the inner core.

Cutting corner blocks from plywood calls for a practical application of geometry, and perhaps a few hints on handling the plywood would not spoil the problem of how to cut the triangles. Begin by ripping the plywood sheet (4' x 8') in half (2' x 4'). This makes it much easier to handle and does not affect the number of corner blocks and keystones one is able to cut out of a sheet.

There are several methods of attaching corner blocks to the flat frame. Nailing is the first method, either *clout nails* or blue lath nails. A *clout nail* is a special soft metal, flat-sided nail designed to curl under when it strikes a hard surface, steel or concrete. The clout nail forms a very secure bond between the corner block and the flat frame. Clout nails, (1¼") are a special kind of hardware available *only* from theatre supply houses. Blue lath nails (1″or 1¼″) are a substitute for clout nails because they are readily available from lumberyards and hardware stores. The 1″ lath nail usually does not need to be clinched (bent over on the front side of the flat); however, the 1¼″ does need to be clinched. When corner block or keystone nails are clinched on the front side of the flat, it is important that they be buried in the wood so that no sharp points are sticking up at any point or they may tear the muslin or canvas covering of the flat when it is sized. A good grade of white glue is usually applied to the down side of the corner block before it is nailed.

Attaching corner blocks and keystones with screws is another method of assembly. Five holes need to be drilled through the block and part way into the stile and rail. Use a ⅛″ bit in either an electric drill or hand-type push drill; this is just about the right size to take the #9, ⅞″ wood screws used to attach the block. The drilling pattern seen in Figure 15 gives strength to the joint. Once all four corners have been attached, the toggle bar is fitted in the center of the wooden frame and attached to the right and left stiles with keystones. Keystones are ¼″ pieces of plywood, about 5″ or 6″ long and 2½″ or 3″ wide, and are attached to the toggle bar and rail with five screws, as are the corner blocks. It is not necessary to use the picture-frame miter clamps on these joints. To test the squareness of the flat, stand it on all four sides; it should stand straight on each side.

Covering the Flat. Covering the flat involves the following steps: (1) laying on the unbleached muslin, (2) gluing and stapling the muslin, and (3) trimming the muslin.

Unbleached muslin is the least expensive and most readily available covering material for flats or screens. Most dry goods and department stores handle unbleached muslin in 36″ and 48″ widths. While these widths are usually too narrow for 5′ flats or screens, they work nicely for narrower flats. Scenic muslin, slightly heavier, comes in 72″ and 78″ widths and is much easier to work. Scenic muslin is cheaper when purchased in bolts of 50 to 70 yards, but it can be bought by the yard from some theatrical supply houses. Any group planning to build a new stock of flats or add a considerable number to its present stock should consider purchasing muslin in bolts rather than by the yard. Several large textile mills in the East run specials on muslin at least once a year, and a school can realize a considerable saving by purchasing at these times. Narrower widths can, in an emergency, be sewed together. A seam will appear in the middle, but this is usually not too noticeable once the flat is painted, provided the seam has been closely stitched. The prime disadvantage in sewing muslin together is that the seam is the first place the flat will come apart. While some scenery makers advocate using canvas, it is not recommended. Canvas is bulky and difficult to work with. In addition, the cost is about twice that of unbleached muslin.

Using 72″ muslin, unroll enough so that about 6″ extend over the bottom and top rails and the left and right stiles. The flat frame should be lying face up on the stage or scene-shop floor. Face up means that the corner blocks and keystones will be resting on the floor. The muslin *should not be pulled tight* but should lie loosely on the frame and slightly off the floor. If muslin is stretched too tightly before it is sized or painted it can warp and twist the entire flat out of shape. A tack or staple should be placed in each of the four corners to hold the muslin in place.

Gluing the muslin to the frame is the next step. Three kinds of glue may be used for this purpose: any of the white glues on the market today, Elmer's or Leech glue (frequently used by art departments), or casein glue. Be certain to spread the glue on *both* sides of the muslin to be glued to the rails and stiles. Mix the caesin glue with water (warm or cold) and spread it on the muslin and wood with a paint brush. Another type of glue is regular hide glue, which must be prepared in a double boiler or a glue pot. The bonding power of hide glue is greater than either the white or caesin glues, but it involves more preparation (soaking and heating) and has a rather unpleasant odor.

The glue is spread along the stile first; then the muslin is pressed down on it and another application of glue is put on the muslin. A piece of scrap lumber about 3″ long will help smooth out the wrinkles. *Be careful not to stretch the muslin or pull it too tightly.* Glue the entire flat first; then staple or tack. The reason for this is to avoid developing wrinkles in the muslin which could show up later. Glue the rails in the same manner as the stiles, making certain the wrinkles are smoothed out completely by pulling the muslin toward the outer edges of the rails. Finally, a row of

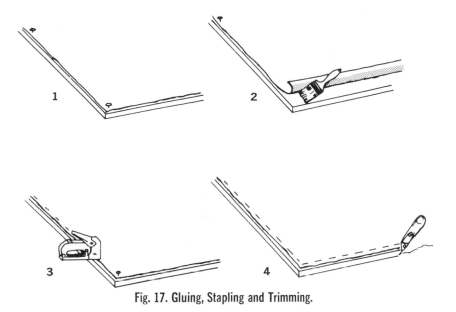

Fig. 17. Gluing, Stapling and Trimming.

tacks or staples about 6″ apart is placed all around the frame, rails, and stiles. *Never glue or tack the toggle bar; let it alone!* It is best to allow eight to twelve hours for the glue to dry properly; so it is advised that all gluing and stapling of muslin be done in one work session. Once the muslin on the rails and stiles has dried, the surplus muslin must be trimmed off ¼″ to ½″ in from the outer edge of the flat with a trim knife or single-edge razor blade (see Figure 17). Make the first cut on the stile and gently pull the surplus as you cut, in order to keep the material taut and make the cutting easier. The pull-cutting operation takes a little practice to get the right amount of tension, but it makes a neatly finished flat. The flats are now ready for the final preparation step, sizing.

Sizing is the process of filling the weave of the muslin fibre with a glue and water mixture to make painting easier. Sizing also shrinks the muslin a great deal and makes the flat tight, like an artist's canvas. Flats that have not been sized before painting may warp and the paint, when applied, will "bleed" through the open weave.

Size water is a mixture of glue and water. The mix is made as follows: one cup of hide glue to one gallon of water. Commercial

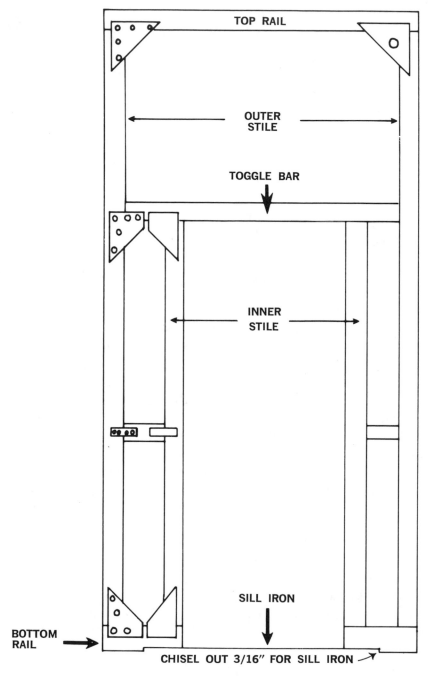

Fig. 18. Door flat.

wall sizing, purchased in most paint stores, will work *if it is thinned* with more water after the directions on the box have been followed. If it is applied according to directions it is too heavy with glue and the muslin becomes hard and brittle. Add water a little at a time to the commercial wall size until the fingers just stick together. Brush sizing on just as though you were painting the flat (see page 35 - 40 for painting instructions). The stage floor, if that is where the painting is to be done, should be protected with a layer of old newspapers or plastic dropcloths. Sized flats should stand for twenty-four hours before applying the base coat of paint.

Door and Window Flats. Door (see Figure 18) and window flats are modifications of the basic flat-construction process. Door and window flats are usually 5′9″ in width, and seldom less than 5′6″. The reason for this is so the door flat or window flat, when used alone as a set piece, does not appear out of proportion.

The major parts of a 5′ 9″ door flat are as follows:

> 2 outer stiles
> 1 top rail
> 1 toggle bar
> 2 bottom rails
> 2 inner stiles
> 2 short toggle bars
> 6 corner blocks, 4 keystones

The top rail and the two outer stiles are assembled as in the basic flat. The long toggle bar is placed so it is exactly 3′ from the top of the top rail to the bottom of the toggle bar. Inner stiles and bottom rails can be assembled as separate units, using the picture-frame miter clamps at all corners. Remember, the stile rests on the rail. The assembled inner stiles are laid in the assembled outer frame. The corner blocks used on the inner stiles need to be trimmed on one corner so they will fit properly without overlapping. Remember to keep the corner blocks ¾″ from the outer edge of the flat. Corner blocks should be trimmed before they are attached to the flat frame. Note that corner blocks are used on the inside, where the inner stile and the toggle bar meet; this is for added strength. Be certain to follow the drill-hole pattern for attaching all corner blocks.

To cover door flats use three pieces of muslin. Lap them on the long toggle bar and use a single row of staples or tacks to ensure that the muslin will not pull loose. After the muslin has been applied and trimmed, as in the basic flat, a "saddle iron" is added to the bottom of the frame. Saddle irons, or "sill irons," can be purchased from commercial theatrical supply companies (be sure to give the exact size of the opening). Saddle irons can be made from 3/16" x ¾" strap iron that is cut 6" shorter than the bottom rails. A sill iron of some nature is necessary to give stability to all door flats.

Window flats are constructed just as the door flat and basic flat, with the following exceptions: (1) the bottom rail is complete—5' 9"; (2) the sill of the window is placed 3' up from the bottom rail; (3) the opening for the window should be 3' x 4'. Assembly of the window flat is the same as for the basic flat or door flat. Extra toggle braces usually are added to window flats at the 5' mark. A window flat can be covered with one piece or with four pieces of muslin, lapping at the bottom and top toggle bars, as was done with the door flat.

It is possible to convert door flats into window flats by using a 3' x 3' plug, made of Upson board, and a wooden frame. The plug should be nailed or screwed to the inner stiles of the door flat, and a "dutchman" is used to cover the cracks. A dutchman is a 5" or 6" strip of muslin that is applied to the flat with paint to hide cracks, such as those made by the plug.

Standardization of door and window flats is not a necessity since the scenery needs will vary from play to play, and many sizes may be used to fit any situation. What has been described here are "stock" sizes.

Door Frames and Window Frames. The door and window flats just described are not complete and ready to place on the stage; a frame to hold the door and windows is necessary for them to be functional. The door frame (see Figure 9) is constructed as follows:

> 2 1" x 6" x 6' 6"
> 2 1" x 6" x 6' 10"
> 1 1" x 6" x 2' 10"
> 1 1" x 6" x 3'

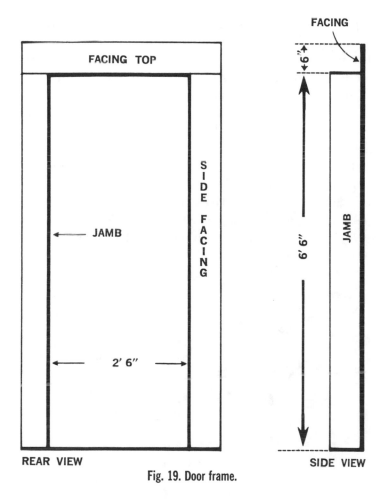

Fig. 19. Door frame.

The door frame is made to be slid in the flat, from the front, so the frame facing rests against the flat. The jamb of the door is the depth the door goes into the flat. The jamb of the door is built by using the two 6' 6" pieces and the two 2' 10" pieces of 1" x 6". The frame should measure 6' 6" *inside,* not outside. Place the 3' piece so it rests on top of the two long 1" x 6"'s. Use either flat L's or mending plates to join the pieces together. The jamb is assembled by using 1½" #9 wood screws and 90° L's (see Figure 20). The jamb is now laid on the floor and the facing frame is laid on top of it. The two units are joined in a butt joint with 1½" #9 wood screws in at least six places on the facing frame . The facing frame will be fragile, so handle it carefully when placing it on the jamb. Once the wood screws are countersunk securely, the unit can be turned over on the facing and more 90° L's are added to hold the two units together firmly. Be careful not to use too many L's on the top as they might block the easy sliding of the door frame into the door flat.

The bottom sill should be beveled with a draw knife or a plane to prevent actors' stumbling over the sill. The door which is attached to the frame is made the same size as the *inside* dimensions of the frame. The door is made of either Upson board or plywood. Upson board is preferable since it is lighter and easier to work, and it is cheaper. The door can be as plain or ornate as one desires. It is best to begin with a plain door and decorate it as needed. The door frame, without the Upson board cover, is

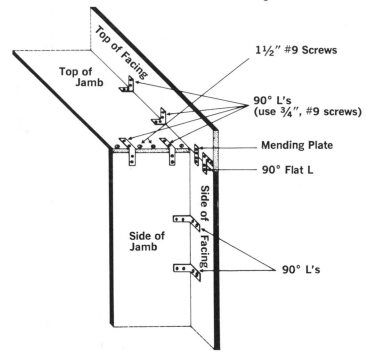

Fig. 20. Door frame assembly detail.

built just as the flat frame was constructed; i.e., top rail and bottom rail are the exact same width and the stiles are shorter than the finished height. The Upson board is then tacked or stapled to the frame. The door is hinged to the door frame with loose pin hinges on the *left side* for door frames going on stage right and on the *right side* for frames going on stage left. *Doors should always open* downstage (to mask the actors' entrance); *doors should be hinged* on the upstage side.

Window frames are constructed in a fashion similar to the door frame, except they are made shorter to fit the window flat. The width of the unit is the same. The height is 3' 8" *inside* the window proper. While some designers make windows that slide up and down, like regular home windows, the author has found that small windowpanes can be designed and nailed to the jamb of the window as need dictates. Regular plaster lath or trellis material may be used to effect a variety of designs from modern to colonial windows. Door or window frames may be held in the flat by several methods. An old-fashioned 6" strap hinge can be placed at an angle on both sides of the jamb so that when it is opened it presses firmly against the flat stile. This method makes shifting the scenery very easy. Another method is to use either 1" x 3" or 2" x 4" blocks, 6" to 8" long, and screw them to the jamb once the frame is in the flat. This method is more permanent and is recommended for single-set plays only. Some stage crews use 90° L's to fasten the frame to the flat. Door and window flats should be braced with stage braces on both sides of the frame. Door frames in flats add considerable weight, and it is necessary to make certain they do not fall. It is not advised to use regular house doors for stage purposes; they are much too heavy and create more problems than they solve.

Platforms. Creating various levels on the stage is one of the most interesting effects a stage crew can produce. Platforms vary in height from 4" to several feet. In the smaller heights, 4" and 6", it is best to build a solid platform using 2" x 4"'s or 2" x 6"'s for the outer frame and the "stringer" support. The author recommends that all platforms be built in terms of a sheet of 3/4" A/D (A/D means one side good, the other side rough) plywood which is 4' x 8'. If platforms are constructed in widths 4' x 8' and 2' x 4', it is possible to use one top for several platforms (sometimes the movable tops are called "lids"). The lids will interchange with the parallel platforms as well.

Tops or lids, made from 3/4" plywood and blocks, are placed on the rough side to prevent the lid shifting once it is on the platform. Tops should be padded with old carpeting, wrong side up, or with layers of newspaper and unbleached muslin. Avoid using any "noisy" substance as a covering material for lids.

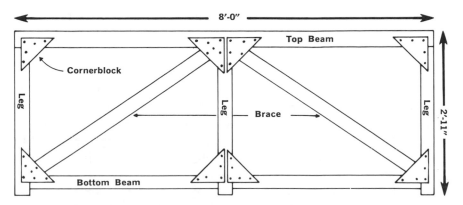

Fig. 21. Sides of the parallel platform.

Parallel platforms usually are constructed in 12", 18", 24", 30", and 36" heights. The design of each is the same, and the leg heights and the braces just increase in size. In Figure 21 the side and end structures are pictured. It is best to join the parallel with more than five screws at the joints. Remember, this structure is designed to give strength without weight. It is constructed of a 1" x 3" of the same quality used in building flats. In Figure 22 the hinging process is illustrated. If this is not followed exactly, the parallel will not fold properly. Drop-pin hinges should be used.

There is a tendency for beginners to build platforms rock-solid with regular construction materials, the 2" x 4"s, 2" x 6"s, and 2' x 8"s used in home building. If you have ample storage space backstage, this is not a bad practice as platforms to hold human beings *should* be strong. However, space limitations and costs should lead stage crews to consider building with lighter materials but constructing so as to gain maximum strength. While parallels of 1" x 3" or 1" x 4" are strong up to a height of three (3') feet, platforms over that height must be built of 2" x 4" or 2" x 6" for sufficient strength and rigidity.

Special Sizes and Shapes. Any size or shape flat, door flat, door frame, or platform can be constructed to meet special needs.

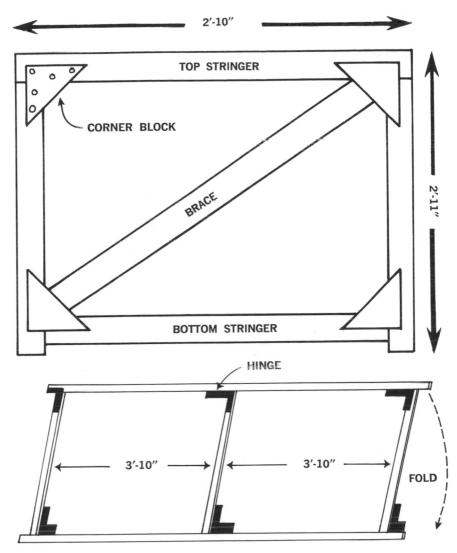

Fig. 22. The hinging process. Above, the ends
and middle of the parallel platform. Below, placement of hinges.

What has been described here are *basic* scenery construction methods and suggestions toward standardization in sizes. Most of the plays to be produced in high schools today are one-set shows requiring such standard items.

Once the scenery is constructed it is ready for painting.

PAINTING

Just as the custodian and the industrial arts teacher were consulted in building scenery, the art teacher should be consulted about painting the set. The design, color, and texture are specialized areas of art, and it is quite likely that the painting crew will not have this specialized kind of knowledge. It is also possible that the director of the play will not have an extensive art education. Of course, *do not hand over the responsibility* of painting the set to the art teacher, merely ask for advice.

Painting scenery involves the following steps: (1) selecting the color or colors of the set, (2) mixing the base coat, (3) applying the base coat, and (4) spattering coats.

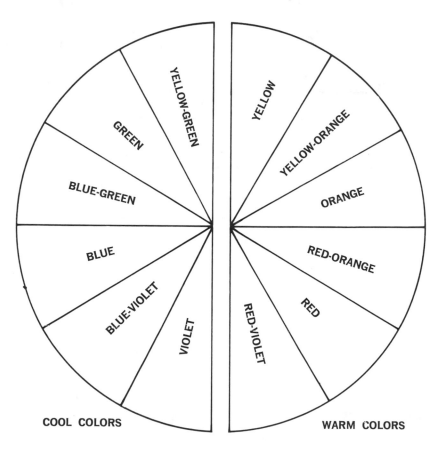

Fig. 23. Color Wheel.

Color. Color is divided into two categories—warm and cool. Warm colors are best suited for comedies, farces, and plays that are not tragic in nature. Cool colors are best suited for serious dramas, mysteries, and classical plays. The color wheel (Figure 23) illustrates the spectrum of warm and cool colors.

The theme of the play should determine the color of the scenery because certain colors denote certain attitudes and feelings.

Yellow: Cheerfulness, gaiety, lightheartedness, sunniness. If *grayed*, it indicates sickness, cowardice, jealousy.

Red: Violence, excitement, rage, danger, wrath, strife. Too much red area on the stage tires an audience quickly.

Green: Restful, youth, growth, faith. It is rather neutral in emotional impact unless it is very intense or blackened.

Purple: Royalty, nobility, death, sadness, and strength of spirit.

Blue: Coolness, serenity, vastness (of distance), aristocratic, nothingness.

Black: Gloom, death, depression. Too much black on the stage can depress an audience, but black, when mixed with other colors, can project *degrees* of gaiety, excitement, coolness, etc.

White: Truth, innocence, purity, chastity. White mixed with other colors also can project *degrees* of attitude or feeling.

Gray: Humility, resignation, old age.

Brown: Earthiness, commonness, poverty, oldness.

It is not possible to present all information concerning color here; however, this little bit of information should stimulate further research into the fascinating study of color. See the art or home economics teacher for added information.

Paint. For many years all scenery was painted with regular artists' dry colors; indeed, many still use them. Frequently, high school scenery or paint crews have great difficulty in mixing dry paint properly; therefore a substitute of suitable quality is desireable.

Most major paint companies produce a waterbase *caesin paint* that can be mixed in almost as many shades as dry color. Mixing caesin paints is much simpler than mixing dry paints. Caesin comes in a very thick consistency (much like butter), and mixing the gallon of base with a gallon and a half of water produces paint of about the thickness of heavy cream, just the right painting consistency. With caesin paints, *no glue need be added* to the mix.

If you use white as the base for nearly all colors, it will be possible to get the exact color desired, and white is rather inexpensive compared to the intense colors of raw umber and burnt
sienna. As in dry color, *a little* intense color *goes a long way;* so
add color slowly.

Caesin paints are readily available from hardware, paint
stores and lumberyards. Scenery or paint crews can mix paint
easily with minimum supervision by the director once the
color and proper proportions have been determined. Mixing
requires three or more 10-quart plastic buckets, a strong paint
paddle, warm water, the base color, and tinting colors. A plastic
measuring cup (one cup or one quart) will help in determining
exact measurements. In the beginning it is wise to *mix more*
paint than you feel you will need. Caesin paints keep for a week
or more if they are covered with a wet towel or rag when not in
use.

Fig. 24. Applying the base coat.

Applying the Base Coat. To apply the base coat of paint, all the flats are laid face up on the stage or the scene-shop floor. One should be certain that a walk space is left between the flats so that painters can walk all the way around a flat. Using 4"—or better still 6"—nylon-bristle brushes, apply the paint by dipping the brush into the paint and wipe the excess off on the inside edge of the paint pail. Care should be taken not to get too much paint on the brush or to dip the brush too deeply in the paint. The paint is applied to the flat in a series of overlapping strokes, in the shape of figure 8's or X's. (See Figure 24) Do not attempt to paint too far with one brushload of paint; dip the brush frequently in the paint.

Painting flats as they lie flat on the floor presents the possibility of puddling—of paint collecting in puddles at various points on the flat, usually near the center above and below the toggle bar. It is best to apply the base coat as you work from the center to the outer rail. Paint applied in figure 8's gives a much better texture than that applied in straight lines. The base coat should be allowed to dry at least twelve hours before any other paint is applied to the flat.

It is best to stir the paint frequently, although caesin paint settles out less than dry-color mixes. If many flats are to be painted, begin painting the flats at one end of the stage and work to the other end; in an hour or two the flats that were painted first have "set" enough that they can be leaned against the back wall of the stage and will take up much less space.

Flats painted with a base coat are *not* complete; they lack texture and depth. To achieve both texture and depth, the flats need another paint treatment. Various methods have been employed by scenic artists to get the proper texture desired; spattering, drybrushing, and spraying are examples.

Spattering. Spattering is one of the time-honored techniques. The brush, having been cleaned in water after applying the base coat, is dipped lightly into the paint color selected as the *first* spatter coat, and the paint is "flipped" toward the flat so that the paint lands in tiny drops. The brush can be struck against a board or hit against the hand. The size of the drops will vary with the amount of paint used—but be careful not to get *too much paint;* this will spoil the entire effect. It is suggested that a practice flat be used for developing the spattering technique.

The color of the first spatter coat should be either a full shade lighter or darker than the base coat but of the same hue. A good rule of thumb is that if the base coat is light, spatter with a darker shade first; if the base coat is dark, spatter with a lighter shade first. The second spatter coat can be applied once the first coat has had time to dry, usually in three or four hours. The second coat should be of an opposite color—across the color wheel from the base color (see Figure 23). Care should be taken not to spatter opposite colors too heavily as they will "turn" the color of the set very quickly. A third and fourth spatter coat can be applied, depending upon the texture desired. To make them look old, spatter them with dark brown and black especially near the top of the flat. Spattering should be fairly heavy.

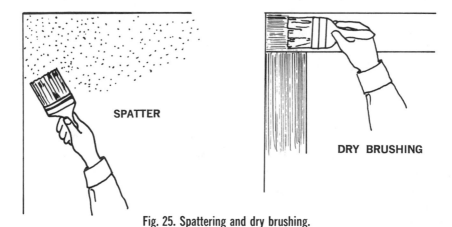

SPATTER

DRY BRUSHING

Fig. 25. Spattering and dry brushing.

Dry-brushing. This texturing technique is particularly useful on woodwork or to produce a woodwork effect. First, the painter must have a *dry* brush. The brush is dipped very lightly in the paint and dragged across the surface to be treated. Dry-brushing is usually done with a single color: dark brown, black, or dark gray. It takes some practice to develop a good dry-brush technique but the effect is well worth the time. (See Figure 25 for effects of spattering and dry-brushing.)

Spraying and Sprayers. Spraying is a quick method of achieving results similar to spattering. The use of hand fly-spray guns is not usually effective. Occasionally one of the more expensive large-capacity models will work for a while, but by and by the nozzle will clog. Paint used in spray guns should be thinned down considerably and stirred thoroughly so that there are no lumps. Spraying should be done 10 to 18 inches from the flat, depending on the kind of gun. The large tank-type garden spray is one of the most dependable kinds of hand-operated sprayers. They are much more expensive to purchase but outlast many of the inexpensive fly-spray guns. The best spray gun is the electric type, and some models are now fairly inexpensive ($7.00 to $12.00). This gun takes practice to use properly but it produces wonderful results. Needless to say, all spray guns should be cleaned completely after each spray coat. Spraying gives a much finer texture than spattering, and more colors can be used. Both spraying and spattering a set can produce some very effective texture results.

A word of caution about paints:

1. Do not use any form of *enamel* or *oil-base* paint on flats (unless you are ready to throw them away after one show). Oil-base paints do not "paint over" on muslin.
2. Do not use spray cans of paint in gold or silver on flats. It is nearly impossible to paint over gold or silver paints.
3. Avoid latex (rubber-base) paints except for door frames and furniture. It builds up on flats, makes them sag, and gives them a shiny appearance under stage lights.
4. If several people on the scenery crew are painting, it is best that they work together and blend their work, since no two people paint alike.
5. No one learns to paint out of a book, this one or any other. Practice is the only way to perfect painting techniques.

PUTTING SCENERY TOGETHER

Once the scenery has been constructed and painted, its placement on stage is the final step. Handling flats is a tricky business for those who have never handled them before, and a few tips are in order.

Too many stage-crew members want to pick up the flat and carry it alone wherever it is needed. Flats should only be carried by *two people,* one at either end of the flat. If you carry a flat alone, you run the dangers of personal injury, cracking the stiles or rails of the flat, ripping or tearing the muslin on other scenery, and knocking down scenery already put up. Keep the bottom rail on the floor at all times and balance the flat with the "high hand" and push it where it is needed. Then wait for the scenery chairman or stage manager to position the flat for assembly.

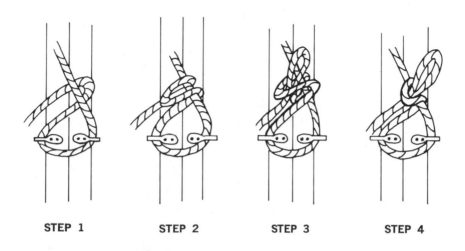

STEP 1   STEP 2   STEP 3   STEP 4

Fig. 26. Lashing Tie-Off.

Lashing flats together is the commonest and simplest method of putting scenery up. Each flat has a length of clothesline attached to the upper right-hand corner (as one looks at the back of the flat). Spaced at regular intervals below the lashline are "lash cleats" (see Figure 15) over which the lashline is thrown or flipped by holding onto the lower end of the lashline and aiming for the top lash cleat with the natural loop created by the throw. Lashing requires a little practice, so crew members should not be discouraged if they miss the lash cleat a few times. Some stage managers or scenery chairmen prefer to lash with the aid of a stepladder. The lashline is then moved from one cleat to the other. The bottom cleats on most flats are called "tie-off" cleats and are somewhat thinner than the regular lash cleat. After all cleats have been included in the lashline, a tie-off is made according to Figure 26. You should remember to keep the lashline as tight as possible during the entire process, including the tie-off. A little practice lashing and tieing-off will make most members of the stage crew proficient after one play.

Nailing scenery together is another method of assembly. Nailing, however, presents a safety problem. To nail flats together in pairs it is necessary to place the flat face down on the stage and use short scraps of 1″ x 3″ as the joiner. It is best if the flats are joined in at least three places—top, bottom, and at the middle above the toggle bar. Occasionally two flats will meet at 90°, more or less, and you can join these by placing a 6-penny nail in the stile at the top, bottom, and middle. Make certain that the nail hits the edge of the stile of flat #2 in this process. It is best not to drive the nail all the way in but to leave just enough of the head out so that it can be removed with a claw hammer. A supply of double-headed nails 6 or 8 d can be kept on hand for this purpose. The nailing method of assembly should not be used if the set is to be changed during the play or if it is necessary to clear the stage for other activities before the actual production date. Since this situation occurs in most schools, it is recommended that the flats be nailed in pairs so the set can quickly be reassembled without repeating the entire nailing process.

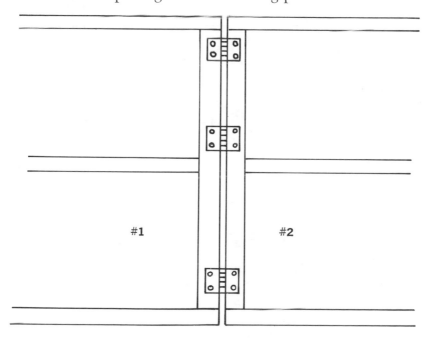

Fig. 27. Hinging flats.

Hinging flats together is a third method of assembly. Drop-pin or loose-pin hinges are used in *all* hinging on the stage (see Figure 29). The reason for this should be quite clear. All flats must come apart for easy storage, and unless the flats are built as two- or threefolds they cannot be folded completely. In putting hinges on the flats for assembly purposes, they must be attached at a standard distance from the top and the bottom of the flat. Flats are not always assembled in the same order for each production, and they should be interchangeable with one another. While hinging has many apparent advantages, cost is not one of them. It will cost at least a dollar to put hinges on each flat. Another disadvantage is that, no matter how hard the stage crew tries, not all flats are going to assemble with hinges alone. Matching up hinges on ten flats so that all interchange is nearly impossible; the set always assembles best the way it was done originally. Hinging works best on twofold and threefold flats, intended to be permanently hinged together. In making this assembly it is necessary to use a "jigger," a 1″ x 2″ strip placed between the two flats to facilitate folding (see Figure 28).

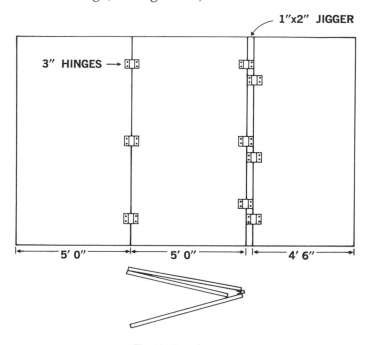

Fig. 28. Threefold flats.

Fig. 29. "Oklahoma," James W. Miller Auditorium, WMU. Directed by William Livingston, designed by Roy Beck.

Large walls may be assembled by using a "stiffener" (a long length of 1″ x 3″) and a "keeper hook" (see Figure 29). The keeper hook is a piece, usually of ½″ wide flat-iron, bent to an S shape to slide over the toggle bar of the flat. In assembling three flats it is necessary to have three keepers, one for each flat, placed in the center of the toggle bar, and the 1″ x 3″ stiffener is dropped in the bottom loop of the S.

Large straight walls of 3 or more flats may be assembled by using a stiffener (a long length of 1″ x 3″) placed across the back of all the flats of the wall and nailed to each individual flat in several places with double-headed nails. Usually two stiffeners are needed to give the wall sufficient rigidity and stability. Care should be taken not to drive the nails through the flat, but in just far enough to secure a bond.

Of the three methods of assembly, lashing is by far the easiest and the cheapest. Clothesline is relatively inexpensive and 8- and 10-penny nails can be substituted for lash cleats if necessary. Stage managers and directors for years have sought to find easier methods, but nearly always they return to lashing as the best way.

Once the entire set is up or the set pieces are in place, the "dutchmanning" process is next. Dutchmanning is adding 4″ or 5″ strips of muslin (dipped in the base paint) to the seams where flats are joined together. The dutchman strip is usually soaked in the base paint so that the paint oozes through the cloth fibers. The strip is then applied to the seam by hand or with a brush.

This is a messy process, and care should be taken to protect the stage floor and the rest of the set. Since dutchmanning is one of the last things to be done to the set, it is frequently omitted. Most audiences will accept a stage setting for what it is: an "illusion" of reality. Well-made flats usually are joined together with a fine seam and dutchmanning should be used only where *extreme* realism is *required*. Permanent two- and threefolds flats should be dutchmanned when they are made; these will be painted as the set is painted and will require no other treatment.

At certain key points all sets need to be braced with stage braces or homemade versions of stage braces (see Figure 30). Entrances require bracing on both sides of the door (hinged and opening). Long flat walls require at least one brace, and frequently the windows need bracing. A commercial stage brace, either of wood or aluminum, lasts for years. The hook at the top of the brace is inserted upside down into the brace cleat on the flat and turned 180° so that the brace rests against the flat stile and the brace cleat. These directions are important! A misapplied brace can ruin weeks of work by ripping through the muslin covering with the first jar the brace gets backstage. The "rocker" end of the stage brace is either screwed to the stage floor with a stage screw or nailed with #10 or #12 nails and toed over. The adjustment in the center of the brace provides for making certain the flat stands straight and does not tilt backward or forward. Be certain the thumb screw is tight once the flat stands straight.

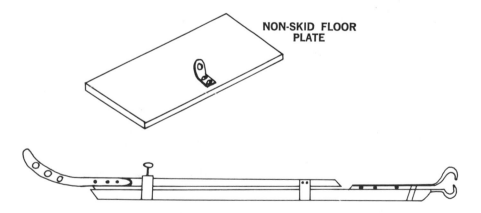

NON-SKID FLOOR PLATE

Fig. 30. Adjustable stage brace.

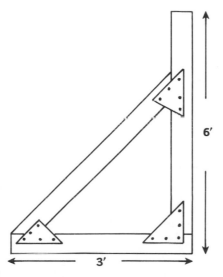

Fig. 31. Scenery Jack.

In many schools nailing into the stage floor or drilling holes for stage screws is strictly forbidden. In other schools the stage floor is made of regular hardwood flooring instead of softwood, as recommended by theatre architects. How does a play-producing group cope with these problems? You can "do it and damn the devil," or you can find another method of bracing the set. One manufacturer of stage hardware (Mutual Hardware Company) has perfected a "non-skid floor plate" for use with stage braces (see Figure 30). These are most useful on hardwood or tile floors. Another method is to build a bracing strip of 2" x 4"'s lagged to the back and side walls of the stage so the set can be braced from the top rail of the flat to the bracing strip.

Other methods of bracing are making pseudo-stage braces of 1" x 3"'s in a T shape and nailing them to the flat stile edge. Set pieces may be braced with a stage brace or may be held upright by means of scenery jacks. A scenery jack is made of 1" x 3"'s in a triangle shape in varying heights, according to the height of the flat or set piece (see Figure 31). The height of the jack is usually twice that of the base, but this may vary according to backstage conditions. Jacks are attached to the flat at the toggle bar with hinges. The flat should be laid face down on the stage and the jack laid on the flat ½" from the bottom rail. The ½" provides space for the flat to rock back and the weight of the flat is carried on the back one-third of the jack. Sometimes jacks are attached to both right and left stiles and sandbags are used to weight them down. It usually is not necessary to nail or screw scenery jacks to the stage floor.

Shifting Sets. Some plays require more than one set and it is necessary to *shift* scenery during the progress of the play. The shifting of any scenery requires detailed planning by the director and the stage crew. Each crew member must know exactly what he is to do to complete the shift. A "shifting chart" is recommended in which each crew member is assigned specific tasks.

There are two basic ways of shifting scenery. First, you can "strike" (take down) set number 1 completely, usually starting at the two downstage sides and removing the set, flat by flat (or unit by unit if flats are nailed or hinged together). If the set has a back wall it may be removed intact and stored on the back wall of the stage. In shifting, care should be taken not to cover up set number 2. Silly as that may sound, it has happened to stage crews in a big hurry to make the shift. The second method of shifting is by placing set number 2 "inside" set number 1. This method is quite effective provided the second set is smaller and requires less acting area than set number 1. In making this shift an entrance is made from the backstage area by removing certain flats of set number 1 near the storage area for set number 2. All furniture and props from set number 1 are removed completely or are pushed far enough back to permit set number 2 to be set up. Work should begin from the point farthest from the backstage entrance to the point nearest the entrance. If large props are used in set number 2 they should be put in *first* and pushed down to the curtain line out of the crew's way until the second set is completely up. The "set within a set" method of shifting is one of the better methods and is the one that should be tried, especially if later action of the play returns to set number 1. *Shifting of scenery must be practical,* not taken for granted!

Sets requiring shifting should not be nailed together—hammering onstage is very disconcerting to an audience. Practice the set shifting at least *twice,* and more if time permits. Shifting should be done as quietly and quickly as possible. Remember, a shift that takes a crew five minutes to make seems like fifteen to an audience seated in a dark auditorium. For very long shifts, planned intermissions to "cover" the shift should be used. Sometimes a musical interlude can help the audience pass the time during scene changes (see section on "Sound Effects").

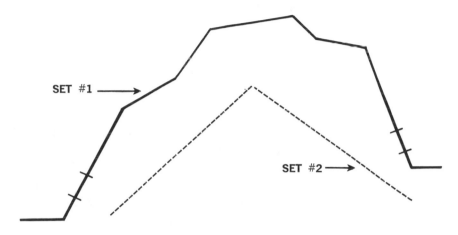

Fig. 32. A set within a set.

Shifting Arena Settings. In arena staging, scene shifts must take place in full view of the audience. No attempt should be made to "sneak" scene changes, but the changes should be made as quickly and quietly as possible. The people making the changes should know exactly what they are to do. They should not put on an "extra performance" for the audience. (Some schools dress all stagehands alike, in coveralls or in costumes of the period of the play.) Stagehands should not wear the "grubbies" usually worn backstage on the traditional stage.

The placement of furniture and large set props can be marked on the floor with masking tape and labeled, or if there are a number of changes, the tape can be color-coded and the pieces marked with a piece of tape of the same color. If changes must be made in darkness or semi-darkness, phosphorescent tape or paint can be used to mark the placement of furniture and props on the stage floor.

Two final words of advice: PLAN and PRACTICE scene changes.

PROPERTIES

Properties are of two basic types: the *large-set property*, which is really a part of the stage setting, and the *small hand prop*. It is the first type that is discussed here. Properties are defined as any part of the stage setting which is movable and not a part of the flats per se. The purpose of properties is to aid the audience in the location and time of the play. You will remember that we said that location and time are the two important functions of scenery. Properties, likewise, serve the same purpose. Set props are usually selected by the properties crew according to a list that appears in the back of most play books. These in part are hand props and in some cases set props. Set props are considered to be the furnishing of the scenery, making the set complete, and as such they should fix the period in which the action of the play takes place. Do not make the serious error of having properties that do not fit the play. Time and again, plays supposedly taking place during the 1900's are furnished with props of the 1950's and 1960's. This is most incongruous and does not aid the audience's understanding of either the location or the time, particularly the time.

Most prop crews are not familiar with all furniture styles, especially period furniture. By consulting one of the leading furniture stores on period styles you will ensure getting the correct style to fit the play. Properties may either be borrowed or made for a particular production. It is recommended that you borrow whenever possible and make properties only as a last resort. It sometimes is necessary to call upon friends of the prop crew in order to supply the furnishings, and many people have stored in their attic, basement, or garage a surplus of furniture. It is on this surplus that a prop crew often must draw. As you begin your work, understand clearly that the furnishings, as hand props, must fit the period of the play. Do not blindly accept the first pieces of furnishings offered to you if you can tactfully refuse. A prop crew should use all the devices at its disposal to locate props. First, contact members of the cast and see if they have the necessary pieces of furniture. Perhaps the director of the play has already located some of the more important pieces. In this case it is up to you to call upon the owners and make arrangements for the props to be moved to the school.

In some cases, if an unusual property is required, it is good publicity to advertise that you need a specific wagon, wheel, or piece of furniture for your play. Not only will it help you in locating the piece but it helps publicize the forthcoming production. The author remembers when the prop crew of a production of *I Remember Mama* advertised for a Model T Ford as Uncle Chris's car. This prop, while not really essential, certainly added flavor to the show, and a series of publicity articles was built around locating the Model T, getting the Model T, and finally pushing the Model T across the house seats onto the stage by means of 2" x 8" planks.

Props and some smaller furnishings do not have to be the real thing. For example, a play calls for a butter churn, but a butter churn can easily be made with a broomstick and a basket. Many times a prop is not seen in its entirety by the audience and therefore may be a facsimile. When set props are vital to the plot of the play it is important to use pieces as authentic as possible.

A few more directions for the property crew. Make a complete list of the properties used, who supplied the props, and carefully note the condition of the props when they are picked up. Labels should be placed on most props to indicate ownership. Sometimes properties become damaged, and it is then your responsibility to tell the director when a property has been damaged and to tell him that the property has a certain value placed on it by the owner. In some communities, furniture stores (furniture is by far the hardest of set props to acquire) will loan furniture to the high school dramatic group. Sometimes this borrowing can be effected by telling the store manager or owner that he will receive due credit on the program along with the cast's and crew's thanks for his contribution to the play. The merchant receives free publicity in the eyes of many playgoers, and stores who loan furniture to a high school group usually are looked upon with favor by all adults.

STAGE LIGHTING

Stage lighting has several important purposes. First of all, an audience comes to *see* a play. Second, in each play there is a certain *mood* which must be conveyed by means of the setting *and* the lighting. Third, lighting should convey *time:* daylight, dawn, night, bright sunlight, etc. Fourth, *special effects* are created by lighting: shadows, lightning, explosions, etc. There are then, four purposes for lighting the stage: *visibility, mood, time,* and *special effects.* An audience should not have to strain to see the actors on the stage, nor should the stage be so brightly lit as to cause the audience to hide its eyes momentarily to avoid eyestrain. While these may seem to be extreme examples, they can happen in your high school play. The happy medium is difficult to achieve in the brief time that you will have to spend in play production.

In order for the four purposes to be conveyed on the stage, two things are necessary: good *equipment* and adequate *control.* Equipment for stage lighting consists of the following lighting instruments: spotlight, floodlights, border lights, and footlights. Control consists of the switchboard and dimming equipment.

The spotlight is the basic lighting instrument that should be used to light the acting areas of the stage, three upstage and three downstage (see Figure 33). "Spots," as they are called, come in four basic types: plano-convex, fresnel, ellipsoidal, and sealed beam.

Plano-convex Spotlight   **Fresnel Spotlight**

Ellipsoidal Spotlight   **Sealed Beam Spotlight**

Fig. 33. Four types of spotlights.

The plano-convex spotlight was one of the first spotlight developments after incandescent lights were introduced on the stage. Its primary features are an aluminum reflector, a globe-shape lamp, and a plano-convex lens. The wattage of the lamp varies from 250 to 2,000 watts. The effective "throw" of the light is from 10 feet to 100 feet. A "hard edge" circle of light is formed by the plano lens. Planos are most effective when hung from the first batten behind the act curtain.

The fresnel spotlight also derives its name from its lens. Its primary features are an aluminum reflector (larger than the plano's), a T-shape lamp, and a lens that has a series of vertical planes and either dots or stripes stippled on the lens. The wattage of the fresnel is usually 500 watts for onstage purposes and up to 1,500 watts for out-front lighting. The effective throw for a 6-inch fresnel on the first batten is up to 25 feet. For the larger fresnels, with 8- and 10-inch lens, the throw is up to 60 feet. The fresnel lens gives the light beam a soft or feathered edge—a clear circle of light is not distinguishable. Six- and 8-inch lens are most effective onstage and 10-inch lens and over serve best from out front.

The ellipsoidal spotlight employs two devices: first is the elliptical reflector and the second is the T-type lamp that burns "base up." By combining the elliptic reflector and the T-lamp the spotlight produces a highly efficient and concentrated beam of light. The beam is directed by a shutter or iris system between the lamp and the lens. Wattage of ellipsoidals, or "lekos" as they are sometimes called, varies from 250 to 2,000 watts, depending upon lens sizes and the throw desired. Lekos serve best from out front and are usually used to light the front acting areas.

The fourth type of spotlight is a recent development: the sealed-beam spotlight. Its origin is largely industrial and "automotive." The headlights of family cars, for example, have sealed beams. Most schools have some kind of outdoor night lighting that employs sealed beams. As the name implies, the lamp and the lens are sealed in one unit. This used to be a disadvantage for use on the stage. By developing new types of lens and filaments, lighting manufacturers were able to refine the sealed beam to satisfy most school stage-lighting needs. Some sealed-beam units employ an additional lens system to increase the output of the unit. Sealed-beam lights may be used onstage or out front. Their effective throw depends on their wattage, which is deceptively low: 75 to 500 watts. The same-watt sealed-beam lamp may be used onstage or out front, and the only adaptation needed is in the length of the light housing: the longer the housing, the longer the throw. The use of another lens system superimposed on the sealed-beam lamp can produce very effective results up to 75 feet.

Sealed-beam lights offer several advantages not provided by traditional stage spotlights. First, they are inexpensive initially, in upkeep, and to burn. Second, they are lightweight and easily handled. Third, lamp replacements are readily available from most local commercial electrical contractors. Schools not having adequate lighting facilities or those planning to remodel older installations should by all means consider sealed-beam lights.

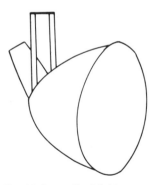

Fig. 34. Scoop flood light.

Floodlights provide light for the stage in a wide angle. Floods are usually used for backlighting and cyclorama lighting. Floodlights do not have a lens system but have reflectors that cover the entire inside surface of the instrument. Floodlights have a short throw, not more than 15 feet effective distance. Floods may be hung from battens or put on light stands. Sky cycloramas and ground rows are usually lit with floods. Occasionally school stages are not equipped with border lights and floodlights are used instead. Various names have been given to floods; "scoops" and "wizards" are two of the more common names.

The long trough of red, white, and blue lights are called border lights. Borders are hung on the stage in two places: on the first batten with the spotlights or immediately behind them, and about the middle of the stage behind the second border curtain. Border lights are made in two basic types: the *continuous reflector* type and the *individual reflector* type. The continuous reflector has a single reflecting surface running the full length of the trough or strip. In the trough are placed colored lamps of from 60 to 150 watts. Individual-reflector-type border lights usually come in sections 6′ to 12′ long and may be hung on the first batten, separated by several spotlights. Each color is individually controlled at the switchboard. A new version of the border light has been recently introduced on the stage in the form of the small-wattage sealed beams, R–40's or PAR's, in a housing that looks like a small spotlight. Wattage varies from 75 to 200 watts.

The purpose of border lights is to give *general illumination,* to *tone* and *blend* the acting areas. While most schools will probably have red, white, and blue lights in the border, the true light primary colors are red, green, and blue. Red, white and blue, when mixed, never produce any light color except those shades of red and blue. However, red, green, and blue, when mixed, produce a wide range of color, from gray to white.

Footlights, while an integral part of older stages, have been almost eliminated from modern lighting installations. If the high school stage is equipped with foots, their use is not recommended for several reasons. First, foots have a tendency to create "skull" effects on the faces of the actors, making the eyes appear hollow and black. If tradition dictates that footlights should be used in the school, it is recommended that they be dimmed *very low.* Today, with modern spotlights and adequate dimming equipment, footlights are relatively useless.

The Dimming Mechanism. The dimming mechanism is next in importance to the lighting instruments. The purpose of the dimmer is to control the *level* of the lighting instruments—the brightness or dimness of the lamps in the spots, borders, and/or floods. The dimmers are usually housed in a complex called the switchboard, in which are located the main toggle switches or circuit-breakers for turning the lights on and off. A number of different-type dimmers are on the market today.

The oldest type, and the least efficient, is the *resistance* dimmer. This system utilizes a number of different-size contacts of various thickness to control the amount of electrical current flowing to the lamps. The thicker the contact the less electrical current; the thinner the contact the more electrical current that flows through. Resistance dimmers are identifiable by their sizes; they are large and have a circle of radial contact points. Resistance dimmers have a number of disadvantages over the newer types. First, they need a certain number of watts to operate, or a *minimum load*, before they operate properly; second, resistance dimmers have a *maximum load* and cannot take overloads. Thus, putting too few or too many lights on the dimmer is a problem. In many cases the dimmers are permanently wired so the load factor is taken care of properly; however, this prevents the flexibility required by today's lighting needs as it limits the number of lighting instruments that can be plugged into a given circuit. If the dimming system is to be replaced (resistance dimmers have a rather short lifespan: 10 to 15 years), schools should consider one of the newer types.

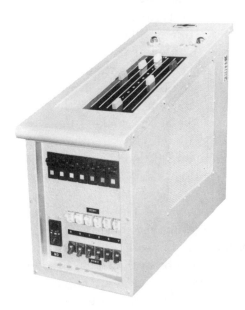

Fig. 35. Autotransformer dimmer.
(Photo courtesy Electro-Controls, Ariel Davis Mfg. Division)

The autotransformer dimmers are another recent development in dimming equipment. As the name implies, the dimming coil resembles that of a transformer, as in model railroads or slot-cars. The advantage of the autotransformer is that it can dim *any size* load up to its maximum rating. For example, it can dim a 25-watt lamp or a total load of 6,000 or 12,000 watts, whichever is the maximum rating. The autotransformer dimmer is lightweight since there are few moving parts; it takes up less space because it is compact; and it is much cooler in operation since the coil does not heat up. (See Figure 35).

The perfection of transistors and miniature electronic equipment has opened a vast new era in lighting technology. Space limitations and the wide variety of new electronic dimming equipment does not permit the author to describe in detail all the newer types. Generally, all modern equipment operates without moving parts and the dimming is done with electronic tubes or amplifiers. Most systems operate on low voltage at the dimming console and the high voltages are contained in the electronic equipment, usually housed backstage or in the stage loft. The new electronic dimmers (See Figure 36) provide for proportional dimming; that is, both a 750-watt lamp burning at full intensity and a 500-watt lamp burning at half intensity can dim out at the same time.

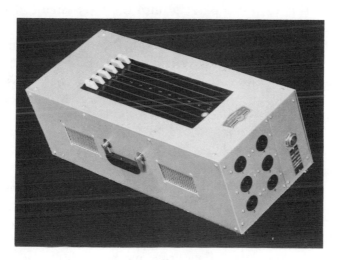

Fig. 36. Electronic dimmer pack.

Response in the new electronic dimmers is almost instantaneous; time is measured in milliseconds. Two of the new electronic dimmers are the silicon rectifiers and the magnetic amplifiers. The silicon rectifier utilizes solid-state circuitry (See Figure 37); the dimmers have a very long life and require little maintenance. The magnetic amplifier features remote-control consoles and instant response, plus low maintenance. Some of these new dimming control boards feature a punch-card system that permits the lighting crew to plan all light changes and put them on electronically sensitive cards. These are then fed into the dimmer control at the proper time. All lighting changes take place electronically. Nearly all of the electronic dimmer consoles feature five or six scenes, preset. This means the lighting operator can set up in advance five or six scenes and then, by throwing a single master lever, light the stage as desired. Changes in stage-lighting technology are taking place so rapidly that any school contemplating installing or adding new lighting equipment should consult representatives of the lighting companies.

Regardless of the type of dimming control used, it is necessary to connect the lighting instrument to the dimming equipment. Most switchboards do this via a patch-panel or quick-connect panel. The principle employed by both is the same. In the patch-panel, a cord is plugged into the dimming circuit the operator wants to use; then it is plugged into the light circuit wanted. All light circuits terminate in a panel, so it is possible to connect any light circuit to any dimmer. The quick-connect panel differs in that no cords are involved in connecting the light circuit to the dimmer circuit. Instead, a series of buss bars, in a crisscross fashion, permit the operator to use a contact slider to connect any two circuits with proper positioning (usually a numbered or lettered stop. See Figure 38).

Permanently wired light circuits usually are the rule in most high schools over twenty years old, and lighting crews are faced with the problem of getting instruments off the circuit or adding more to it. There is a method for adding more instruments without taxing the dimming unit's capacity. The branch-off connector can be used in most schools by lowering the wattage of the existing lighting instruments and adding another lighting device to make the total wattage equal that of the initial wattage specifica-

Fig. 37. Silicon Rectifier.

tion. Sometimes it is necessary to cut cables of permanently wired circuits to get more flexibility, but this should be done only by a qualified electrician or school maintenance staff.

Fig. 38. Quick-connect panel.

Lighting Plot. Figure 39 represents a basic method of lighting the six acting areas. The upstage areas are lit from the first batten and the downstage areas are lit from out front. This is *basic* lighting, and special requirements for each play will require additional lights.

A "lighting plot" shows the location of lights, the color of each instrument, the area at which it is directed, wattage amounts, and the special effect for which it is to be used. Plots should be worked out with the costume and make-up crews so that the color media do not clash with or "wash out" costume or make-up color. Most lighting plots are tentative to begin with and are finalized during dress rehearsals and technical rehearsals. Before every play the light crew should determine the lighting needs of the play and make out a lighting plot.

Setting Lights. At least three people are necessary to set lights properly. One person, the director or light-crew chairman, should "walk" the acting areas to make certain the lights are set at the right level. With a crew member on the control board and one on a ladder, the upstage lights should be set for up-and-down movement by loosening the large thumbscrews or hex bolts on either side of the spot. For right-left moves there may be either a 9/16″

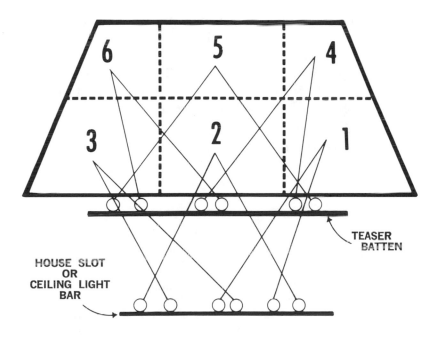

Fig. 39. Cross Spotlighting.

hex-head bolt or a ¾″ nut on a pipe. The man sitting on the ladder should have a pair of leather-palmed gloves and either vise-grip pliers or an adjustable wrench. The person "walking" the areas should fix his gaze at the light and look for the filament in the light. Once the filament is located (this takes practice and experience), it should be centered so that the viewer sees circles or rings as he gazes at it. At this point, the highest intensity to be used on this light during the show should be tested. Once the light is set, the color frame should be inserted so that the walker can get an idea as to proper color media. After each area is set the third man, on the control board, either dims out or turns off that area and brings up the next area. Front lights are set in the same way, with the man sitting either in the "slot" or on a scaffold. Setting the lights takes *time;* it should *not* be left until dress rehearsal. Once all areas are set, the walker should check for dark spots or unwanted shadows. If the area is lit properly, there should be two shadows of him in the light pool from 60° to 90° apart.

Having developed a lighting plot and set the lights, the crew should make a light-cue sheet, noting the lighting changes required and specific instructions by the director for each scene or act of the play. Every member of the light crew must know his specific job during the play. Here is a sample light-cue entry.

LIGHTING CUE SHEET

Act I, Scene 1

Cue:	Change:
George: But Tom, it is impossible.	BLACK OUT: Take down 1, 2, 3, 4, 5, 6 dimmers completely.
Tom: Hey! What happened?	
George: Storm must be heading our way.	SOUND CUE: Thunder.
Cues may be lines, as above, or movements such as: George walks DR; flips switch.	LIGHTNING: Flash switch 21 on and off rapidly.
	Bring all dimmers up to 8½.

Running Lights and Hints for Operators. 1. Lights should move up and down smoothly, not too rapidly. The human eye opens and closes at various speeds, depending on many factors. Consider the comfort of the audience seated in a darkened auditorium.

2. House and stage lights should dim up and down at about the same time for intermissions or at the end or beginning of an act. *Timing is very important.* An audience should not have to wait for the light man to find the house lights' switch or dimmer.

3. Opening the curtain and bringing up the stage lights should occur at the same time. As the curtain opens (assuming it opens on a fully lighted stage) the lights should come up so that when the curtain is fully open the lights are up to the proper dimmer reading.

4. Beware of scenes too dimly or too brightly lit. If the set and furnishings are of "warm" colors, lights should as a rule be dimmed down a very small amount.

5. *Practice light changes* so they come off smoothly and quietly, particularly if the switchboard is located backstage where noise can be heard by the audience.

6. Check out all lights before each performance. Sometimes key spots have shifted or moved because of curtain pulls or other events on the stage during the day. Occasionally lamps have burned out. The checkout should be early in the evening, before the audience arrives.

7. Run lights during rehearsals to give actors the feel of working under lights.

8. Check the switchboard after each performance to make sure it is completely *off*. Leaving a board on "dimmed down"all night can cause damage to dimmers, as well as being a fire hazard.

Running the lights is a big responsibility. Lighting crews should accept this responsibility and make certain that all equipment is kept in good operating condition at all times.

Arena Lighting. Unless your school is equipped with an arena stage and lighting facilities designed for it, you will have to make do with what lighting equipment is at hand. Some of the things about to be suggested can be kept and used again and again for arena productions. Others will work for a single show and can be returned to the lender. You will have to adapt the suggestions made here to your school's physical facilities, for it is not possible to discuss all situations in this volume. But a word of caution—audiences are fickle. Experiment with arena staging, by all means, but do not spend large sums of the dramatics budget on permanent equipment until you see whether or not the theatre-going community accepts arena productions.

To make what is at hand function as an arena lighting system, the following suggestions are made for using the gym floor as the arena.

1. Lighting poles can be made quickly from the volleyball standards used by the P.E. department. Poles can be placed at four points, usually one at each corner of the arena or at the en-

trances to the acting area. Lighting instruments can be placed on the stands 6″ to 8″ apart, or with just enough space to permit focusing. Once the instruments are on the poles, *be sure to weight the base* with sand bags or concrete blocks. The electric lines from the lights can be connected to a portable dimmer (as pictured in Figure 34) or if the stage is located in the gymnasium they can be connected to the regular switchboard. Lights should be focused on the major acting areas and care must be exercised to keep the light out of the audience's eyes. If it is not possible to light the area from one pole, try switching the area lights until you have the desired effect (without lighting the audience as well).

2. Mounting on basketball goals. Long throw spots (40′ or more) can be mounted on the backboards of basketball goals by using blocks of wood 1″ x 3″ and 2″ x 4″ where the C clamp makes contact. This will not hurt the backboard. Another method of mounting on the basketball goal is to raise the basket (quite a number of baskets are on a winch system) and mount the lights on the "locking bar" on the bottom of the basket. Again, you may need to use blocks to make the C clamp secure.

Fig. 40. "Cat on a Hot Tin Roof," Laura V. Shaw Theatre, WMU. Directed by Robert L. Smith, designed by Vern Stillwell.

Methods 1 and 2 are makeshift; they involve a great deal of creative imagination on your part to work out the details. They require the cooperation of custodians and the P.E. department, and plenty of stage cable to make the long runs.

Another item that can be used is a pipe grid, hung from the gym ceiling by trapeze and ring ropes. The grid can be constructed of four 10′ lengths of 1½″ i.d. and four 90° elbows. This grid costs about $20 for pipe but it will last for years. Be certain the grid is adequately balanced and all knots or wire clamps are secure. An operation of this nature must be undertaken *only* under the supervision of the head custodian and the P.E. coach.

Light poles similar to volleyball standards can be built. Make them taller than the volley ball stands, using 1½″ i.d. pipe. These can be made by plumbing shops, or if you are familiar with pipe cutting and threading, the stands can be made in the school shop. The bases of the stands are about 3′ (four lengths of 1½′ pipe), and four 90° elbows are used for feet. The stand requires a four-way tee. For stability with this size base, the height of the upright pipe should not exceed 12′.

It is, of course, possible to mount lights in many other ways for arena productions. Look around your school and locate places for mounting lights for arena productions.

Focusing lights in arena productions is a most important operation. Without borders to blend the areas, a number of shadows will be created using only spots. Unless these detract from the play's action, they should not be of major concern. The color media (gels) can be the same as for the traditional stage, warm colors from the actors' right and cool colors from the actors' left. This should depend on the *major* center of action. Extremely intense colors should be avoided in arena productions: magenta, deep amber, and the pure colors red or green.

SOUND EFFECTS

A classic joke in the theatre illustrates the critical importance of timing sound effects. The villain pulls his gun from his pocket and says: "Charlie, I'm going to shoot you!" He squeezes the trigger, but nothing happens. "Charlie, I'm going to *shoot* you!" Again, nothing happens. "Charlie, I'm going to shoot you," the villain repeats louder, looking anxiously toward the wings. Still nothing happens. "All right, Charlie, I'm going to stab you," the villain shouts, pulling out his pocketknife and rushing toward Charlie. At this moment a loud shot is heard backstage. Sound effects are critical to any production and they must take place *on time*.

Sound-Cue Sheet. Your first duty as a sound-crew member is to make out a cue sheet, much like the lighting-cue sheet, and frequently your sound-cue sheet will be a part of the light-cue sheet. To make your sound-cue sheet, merely substitute the sound effect desired for the lighting change. Experience has shown that if one person makes out the cue sheet, it works better than having many persons do it. Sound crews, by the way, need not be big crews; two or three people with a knowledge of electronics and a good sense of timing can form an efficient team. Once the cue sheet is made, the sound crew is ready to "gather" the sounds necessary for the production.

Bells, Chimes, and Buzzers. Relatively few plays have been written that do not involve either a telephone ring or a doorbell. Every school should have a bellboard, a length of 1″ x 10″ or 12″, containing the following: a doorbell, a buzzer, a door chime, and a 6-volt transformer with a regular house plug on one side of the transformer. For each sound produced there is a separate pushbutton with one wire to the transformer and one wire to the bell, buzzer, or chime. The bell board is carried to the place backstage from which the sound is to originate, or is kept in a central location, usually near the lightboard. The board is plugged into a 110-volt outlet and, on cue, the correct button is pushed.

Sound-crew members must be able to see all of the acting area at all times because many sound cues are moves rather than oral cues. If a play lacks comic relief, just keep ringing a phone after the actor has picked up the receiver. Sound cues must be well timed. Crew members should listen to real telephones and note the length of the ring and the pause between rings. Telephone bells and doorbells can be one and the same sound, with the telephone rings shorter than the doorbell rings. Sound effects must be rehearsed for perfect timing. Just as the cast rehearses four to six weeks on lines, the sound crew should rehearse effects at least two weeks before the production. Good things are not achieved in one or two rehearsals the week of the production.

Recordings. Today, nearly every sound that one can imagine is available on a record. Several major companies supply sound-effect records (they are listed on page 81). It is best to write for a catalogue rather than request a specific sound. Records usually are made with a number of sounds on one side, and a school can save money by studying the most-needed sounds on a single record. Several companies produce a "general" sound-effects record of fairly good quality at a reasonable price.

Tapes. Sound effects also are available on tape, as well as on disc recordings. Tapes do not scratch (one of the biggest problems with discs) and their life is considerably longer. Many publishers feature rented tapes with professional music and sound cues for certain plays.

Live Sounds. Some sound effects are best handled "live"; that is, by producing the sound as it is needed by using the real sound rather than a recording. A gunshot happens to be one that is best produced live. In some states, discharging firearms of any kind, even blanks, is forbidden by law. If a gunshot is required by the play, it is best to check with the local police department concerning these laws. The guns used in track or football work very well. Some theatrical supply houses feature inexpensive blank guns for this purpose, and it is best to buy "soft report" blanks since stages have a tendency to amplify the sound. If state law forbids the discharge of blank guns or the local community has such laws, gunshots can be produced very effectively by using a length of 1" x 3" (6' or 7' long) and placing the foot about 8" to 10" from its end and lifting the other end about 1½' or 2' off the stage floor. Keep it tight and the tension firm; then let it fly! It sounds like a shot. Door knocks, shouts, crowd noises, etc., can all be done live backstage. Be sure to rehearse them, but don't let crowd noises or shouts drown the actors' lines.

Tape-Recorder and Record-Player Hook-up. In Figure 40 the method of hooking up a tape recorder and record player into the auditorium public-address system is shown. The broken line presents an alternate method. Here are several suggestions for using either tapes or record players.

1. Set the volume level on the public-address amplifier, not on the tape or record player. Mark the volume setting with a piece of tape.

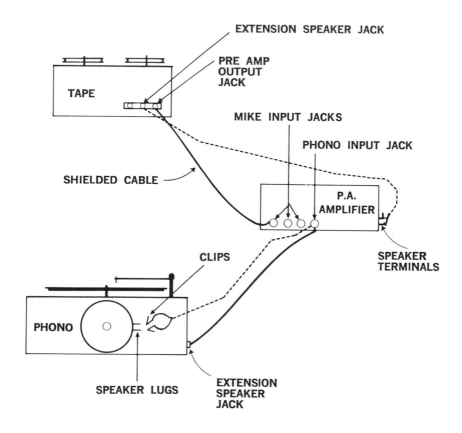

EXTENSION SPEAKER JACK

PRE AMP
OUTPUT
JACK

TAPE

MIKE INPUT JACKS

PHONO INPUT JACK

SHIELDED CABLE

P.A.
AMPLIFIER

CLIPS

SPEAKER
TERMINALS

PHONO

SPEAKER LUGS

EXTENSION
SPEAKER
JACK

Fig. 41. Hooking up tape recorder and record player to public-address system.

2. Turn the P.A. volume down the instant the sound cue is finished. Don't touch it again until the next cue. The motor's running in either the tape or the record player can be picked up readily by the P.A. system. Fade the sound in at the proper moment by turning up the volume on the P.A. system. It takes practice to learn the fading in and out, but it is worth it.

3. Set the volume level on the tape recorder or record player *once* in the beginning, and don't touch it until the play is over. The tape or record player acts as a pre-amplifier for the system and therefore the gain need not be very high.

4. Set the tone level on the P.A. and the tape or record player at about the same place. Treble rather than bass produces

more accurate sound effects.

5. Practice the sounds early in rehearsals so that actors and technicians get the "feel" of sound cues. Just as the actors practice lines, the sound crew must practice sound effects.

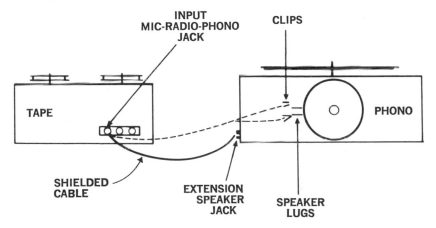

Fig. 42. Connecting a tape recorder to a record player for dubbing.

Dubbing Sounds from Record to Tape. Figure 41 illustrates two ways of connecting a tape recorder and a record player for dubbing. The broken line indicates the method to be used if the record player does not have an extension speaker jack. Sometimes it is necessary to remove several screws to gain access to the speaker lugs under the turntable. These can be replaced once the clips have been applied to the speaker lugs. The clips *must* not *touch each other* or the sound will be distorted with a hum.

1. Find the spot on the record where the sound effect begins, stop the record with your hand, leave the record player on so the turntable continues to spin—even though the record is not. Now *gently* turn the record back one full turn for LP records. The sound effect is now "cued." Hold the record on cue.

2. Depress the record lever on the tape recorder, and hold the tape with the pause lever or button. Volume should be set.

3. Release the pause lever and the tape should travel 6" to 1' at 7½ i.p.s. speed.

4. Release the cued record and record the sound effect.

5. Fade out the volume on the tape recorder when the sound effect is finished. Fade out quickly.

6. Keep the volume level on the record player low to avoid distortion.

7. Stop the tape by pulling the pause lever first; then push the stop button. Pushing the stop button first can cause a "pop" on the tape.

8. Cue the next effect. Allow about 2′ of tape between the sound effects with the volume set at 0 as a leader. Some sound crews give themselves oral cues in the leader space, such as "Sound #2, Act I, car door opening." If oral cues are used it means the sound technician will need a set of headphones to hear the cues. Still others splice in white leader tape as a means of separating sounds. It is possible to write on the white leader the data needed for the cue.

The development of inexpensive 8-track and cassette systems makes either or both tempting for schools to use in sound systems rather than expensive reel-to-reel tape recorders. Both the 8-track and the cassette have major disadvantages for use as sound effects recorders. First, they both travel at slow speeds as compared to reel-to-reel recorders where speed can be adjusted; second, traveling as slowly as they do a very small space is used for the actual sound on the tape, making selections very difficult to locate and more difficult to splice. Certainly the quality of the sound is equal to that of many reel-to-reel recorders, but the disadvantages should be weighed very carefully before investing in an 8-track or cassette system. Either cassette or 8-track is fine for mood music or intermission and pre-curtain music.

Intermission and Scene Change Music. Some schools use music to cover scene changes and at intermissions to give the audience something to occupy its time. Music can assist in creating the proper mood for a play. Further, it helps the audience relax and become more receptive to what will take place on the stage.

Pre-curtain music, played before the play starts, should be of the "mood" type, non-vocal and not the popular music of the moment. Some theatrical supply houses carry a full line of mood music for this purpose. Music should be selected that blends with

the play in terms of *time* and *mood*. Many high school students'
LP collections have music by Percy Faith, Stanley Black, Man-
tovani, 101 Strings, and others that will be suitable for pre-curtain
music.

Fitting the music to the mood of the play is indeed difficult.
Any director or student crewmen thinking of doing this should
begin the "music search" almost as soon as the play is selected for
production. Many times parts of classical works serve well for
climax points and provide unidentifiable themes. These blend well
with many of the classic tragedies. Music used as scene change-
cover also should be of the non-vocal, non-pop kind. Classics,
light opera (non-vocal), and some of the "standards" make the
best scene change-cover. Music should be put on tape at the same
level as the sound effects in order to keep a constant level on the
P.A. volume.

If a school has difficulty locating a specific sound effect, it is
suggested they call on the local radio station for assistance. Most
stations subscribe to a production-aids service that provides nearly
every sound possible. Stations usually are willing to help high
school drama groups, provided they don't wait until the last min-
ute. Be sure you provide the station with a very specific request
and supply a clean tape upon which the sound effect can be re-
corded. Good public relations dictates that the sound technician
making the request for a sound effect provide a couple of compli-
mentary play tickets to the announcer or staff person doing the
dubbing.

Finally, remember that perfection in sound effects is necessary
for every production—comedy, drama, melodrama, farce, or trag-
edy. Practice sound effects in the early stages of production. Dub
as much as possible on tape for ease of handling and reproduction.
Practice timing many times on difficult cues. Be sure to keep the
equipment in good operating condition and return all borrowed
equipment immediately after the final performance.

Fig. 43. "A Clearing in the Woods," Laura V. Shaw Theatre, WMU. Directed by Robert L. Smith, designed by Roy Beck.

STAGE AND LIGHTING TERMINOLOGY

Acting area: the portion of the stage used by the actors during the play.

Act curtain: the curtain hung upstage of the apron, which opens and closes or rises up and down at the end of each act or scene.

Apron: the section of the stage between the act curtain and the orchestra pit.

Asbestos: the fireproof curtain hung in front of the act curtain, closing off the stage area in case of fire; frequently controlled by the fire-alarm system of the school.

Backing: flats or drops behind scenery openings to hide the backstage area.

Backdrop: a large piece of muslin or canvas hung at the back of the stage setting. It sometimes features a painted scene.

Batten: a long piece of wood or pipe from which scenery and lights are hung, and also used for weighting the bottoms of drops.

Border: a width of material hung across the stage above the acting area to hide the grid and loft from the audience.

Border lights: rows of lamps in a long trough, hung by chains or pipes from a pipe batten above the acting area.

Box set: a two- or three-wall setting composed of flats resembling a room interior.

Brace: a jointed, adjustable pole-like support for door flats and window flats.

Cable: 14–2 stranded wire insulated electrical cord for connecting lights to the switchboard.

Circuit: the complete path of electrical current from the outlet to the light instrument.

Color frames: metal holders into which color media is placed and fitted into the front of lighting instruments.

Connectors: devices for joining lighting instruments and stage cables together.

Curtain line: the line on the stage floor the act curtain touches when it is closed.

Cyclorama or cyc: a background curtain hung around three sides of the stage, either smooth or pleated.

Dimmer: an electrical instrument which controls the amount of electrical current flowing to the light instruments.

Flat: a wooden frame covered with muslin or canvas.

Floor plan: a drawing showing the placement of props and scenery on the stage.

Fly: to raise scenery into the loft, out of the audience's view.

Fresnel: an efficient modern spotlight, featuring a lens with concentric circles and producing a soft-edge light.

Gelatin or gels: transparent color media placed in color frame-holders to give the light color.

Grid: a series of I-beams just under the stage roof to which are attached blocks or sheaves through which lines (wire cables) pass to raise and lower battens.

Ground cloth: a muslin or canvas covering for the floor of the acting area, frequently painted a neutral gray or green.

Ground row: low-profile pieces of scenery (shrubs or flowers) used to hide the bottom of the sky cyc or drop.

Jog: a narrow flat, usually less than 2′ wide.

Lash line: clothesline cord used for putting flats together.

Legs: pieces of the cyc, usually 4′ to 6′ wide, hung in pairs running parallel to the act curtain, stage right and stage left, for masking entrances or the backstage area from the audience's view.

Light plot: a drawing or diagram showing the placement of lighting instruments, the plugging systems, and where the light beams hit the stage.

Load: the wattage of light instruments supplied by one electrical circuit.

Parallel platform: a folding platform 12″ to 3′ high.

Profile: an irregular shape in scenery, usually less than 6′ high, such as ground rows, building outlines, suggested walls, and skylines.

Proscenium: the "picture frame" enclosing the stage, the opening between the stage and the audience.

Rake: to slant a setting at an angle from the audience viewpoint.

Return: pieces of scenery used down right and left to mask the backstage area.

Spotlight: a lighting instrument, encased in a metal housing, which gives a beam of light which can be directed and adjusted toward the stage acting area.

Strike: to take down a set or remove a prop from the stage acting area.

Switchboard: the service panel which contains the switches or circuit-breakers controlling the stage lighting; sometimes contains the dimming mechanism as well.

Teaser: a short curtain hung behind the acting curtain, regulating the height of the stage opening and hiding the spotlight batten. Some stages contain three teasers. (Sometimes called *borders;* however, borders are usually fixed and do not move up and down)

Throw: the distance from the lens of the lighting instrument to the object to be lit; most light instruments have a *limited* throw, depending upon wattage.

Wagons: platforms about 6″ high, on casters so they can be moved quietly onstage; width varies from a few feet to 10 or 20 feet.

Wattage: electrical power measurement for spotlights, and lamps; usually denotes capacity or rating by fire underwriters (UAL).

STAGE, SCENERY, LIGHTING, PROPS, AND SOUND EFFECTS ACTIVITIES

1. Make plans to convert the school cafeteria into an arena theatre. Planning should include location of the acting area, seating plan, storage of tables and chairs, entrances and exits, make-up and costume changes, and handling the audience.

2. Plan a profile set for one of last year's plays. Draw a floor plan and a simple perspective.

3. Read the one-act dramatization of Nathaniel Hawthorne's *The Minister's Black Veil* (by Robert Brome) and plan a profile setting for it. Be sure your set conveys the period of the play.

4. Draw a floor plan for Shakespeare's *The Comedy of Errors*. Plan for scene shifts. Show on your floor plan how to accomplish these. Try color-coding the scenes.

5. Plan to add a "thrust stage" to your present stage. How can this be accomplished? Show how it can be made "portable." How can this be accomplished in an auditorium-gym combination—with basketball practice, orchestra rehearsals, etc.?

6. Make a set of model flats about 30" or 36" high. Construct all flats as they should be made. Paint them a neutral gray as a base coat and spatter with each color of the wheel. Plan a set using your model.

7. Make a lighting plot for Tennessee Williams' *The Glass Menagerie*. Note the special-effects lights that are required.

8. Clean and repair all lighting instruments on your stage. Check lamps in spots for "bubbles" (when the lamp is too close to the reflector the glass will mold itself to the shape of the reflector). Check all cables and connectors for loose wires and breaks. Carefully clean the lens systems with paper towels or newspaper (avoid lint left by cloth).

9. Plan a lighting demonstration for your drama club. Use the 3' model set constructed in activity 6 to show the effects of light-color media (gels) on various set colors. Show how the light placement affects mood and meaning on the stage.

10. Work out a property list for the play *RUR* by Karel Capek. (This play can be found in a number of play collections). Be sure to list the props act by act. Make a "prop flow-chart" showing the location and placement of props on the stage. Try making up a code for props and locations.

11. Make a *papier-mâché* prop for Eugene Ionesco's *The Bald Soprano*. Props for this play should be gaudy, surrealistic, and oversize. How else can the prop be made? With what kind of materials?

12. Plan the sound-effects cue sheet for *The Glass Menagerie*. Note the musical cues that run in and out of the entire play. Can this play be made into a dramatic non-vocal opera so that each character has a theme? Locate all suitable sound and musical effects. Make a list of the record numbers and the cut number on the recording.

13. Practice dubbing sound cues with a tape recorder and record player. Practice until you can stop the instant an effect is finished.

14. Visit your local radio station to see how commercials are "cut." Ask to watch while one is being made. Check with the program director about dubbing sound effects for your play.

15. Make a model set for one of the following plays, using cardboard flats and doll furniture: *You Can't Take It with You, The Skin of Our Teeth, The Adding Machine, Gidget, Antigone,* and *Oedipus Rex.*

16. Write to several lighting companies for their catalogues. Make plans to revise your school's lighting system with one of the newer systems. Consult with your director on some of the shortcomings of the present system. Show a complete plan and cost sheet (excluding installation) for all equipment.

17. This activity is a confidence builder for students who are unfamiliar with tools and construction. Working in pairs, measure, cut (with a handsaw), and put together a "test flat" measuring 4' × 3'. After you have made the frame, you are to cover it with a scrap piece of muslin.

18. Collect pictures from home-furnishings magazines and show by floor plan and perspective how you could convert them into stage settings.

19. Consult a book on furniture styles from your high school library or public library. Plan a demonstration on the chief characteristics of various historical periods of furniture. If your libraries do not have such a book, visit one of your town's furniture stores.

20. Make a "production work-schedule" for scenery, lighting, props, and sound effects. Show such items as when set construction begins, when painting of the set is to begin, when the lighting crew should have its plot finished, when they set lights. Get a calendar and a copy of the rehearsal schedule before you start your planning. Resolve such difficulties as rehearsals and work sessions at the same time, and other groups wanting to use the stage or the school shop. Give each crew a deadline by which work is to be completed. Plan to get large props to the school via a truck.

BIBLIOGRAPHY

Adix, Vern. *Theatre Scenecraft.* Anchorage, KY: Children's Theatre Press, 1956.

Bay, Howard. *Stage Design.* New York: Drama Book Specialists, 1974.

Bellman, Willard F. *Scenography and Stage Technology: An Introduction.* New York: Thomas Y. Crowell Co., 1977.

Bowman, Wayne. *Modern Theatre Lighting.* New York: Harper & Row, 1957.

Boyle, Walden. *Central and Flexible Staging.* Berkeley: University of California Press, 1956.

Bryson, Nicholas L. *Thermoplastic Scenery for the Theatre.* New York: Drama Book Shop Specialists, 1970.

Burris-Meyer, Harold, and Cole, Edward C. *Scenery for the Theatre.* Rev. ed. Boston: Little Brown & Co. 1975.

Cornberg, Sol, and Gebauer, Emanual. *A Stage Crew Handbook*. Rev. ed. New York: Harper & Row, 1957.

Daniels, George. *How to Use Hand and Power Tools*. New York: Popular Science Publishing Co., 1965.

Gillette, Arnold S. *Stage Scenery: Its Construction and Rigging*. Rev. ed. New York: Harper & Row, 1960.

Gruver, Bert. *The Stagemanager's Handbook*. Edited by Frank Hamilton. New York: Drama Book Specialists, 1972.

Hake, Herbert. *Here's How: A Guide to Economy in Stagecraft*. New York: Harper & Row, 1958.

Hughes, Glen. *Penthouse Theatre*. Rev. Ed. Seattle: University of Washington Press, 1953.

McCandless, Stanley R. *A Method of Lighting the Stage*. 4th ed. New York: Theatre Arts, Inc., 1958.

Mielziner, Jo. *Designing for the Theatre*. New York: Athanaeum, 1965.

Miller, James Hull. *The Open Stage*. Chicago: Hub Electric Co., 1965.

Parker, W Oren, and Smith, Harvey K. *Scene Design and Stage Lighting*. 4th Ed. New York: Holt Rinehart & Winston, 1979.

Pecktal, Lynn. *Designing and Painting for the Theatre*. New York: Holt Rinehart & Winston, 1975.

Philippi, Herbert. *Stagecraft and Scene Design*. Boston: Houghton Mifflin Co., 1953.

Rubin, Joel, and Watson, Leland. *Theatrical Lighting Practice*. New York: Theatre Arts Books, 1954.

Selden, Samuel, and Rezzuto, Tom. *Essentials of Stage Scenery*. New York: Appleton-Century-Crofts, 1972.

Sellman, Hunton D. *Essentials of Stage Lighting*. New York: Appleton-Century-Crofts, 1972.

Stern, Lawrence. *Stage Management: Guidebook of Practical Techniques*. Boston: Allyn & Bacon, 1974.

Periodicals:

Lighting Dimensions, Cardiff Publishing, P.O. Box 1077, Skokie, IL 60077.

Theatre Crafts, Rodale Press, Inc., 33 East Minor St., Emmanus, PA 18049.

Theatre Design and Technology, U.S. Institute for Theatre Technology, 245 West 52nd Street, New York, NY 10019.

SOURCES OF SUPPLY

1. General Supply Houses: Firms carrying many kinds of theatrical supplies: make-up, hardware, lighting, curtains, etc. Most firms publish catalogs that can be requested.

American Scenic Co.
P.O. Box 283
Greenville, SC 29602

Hoffend & Sons, Inc.
5-45 49th Ave.
Rochester, NY 11101

Mutual Hardware Corp.
5-45 49th Ave.
Long Island City, NY 11101

Norcostco, Inc.
3203 N. Highway 100
Minneapolis, MN 55422

Olesen Co.
1535 Ivar Avenue
Hollywood, CA 90028

Paramount Theatrical Supplies
575 8th Ave.
New York, NY 10018

Tech Theatre, Inc.
P.O. Box 401
Naperville, IL 60540

Theatre Production Service, Inc.
26 South Highland Ave.
Ossining, NY 10562

Theatre Service and Supply Corp.
1792 Union Ave.
Baltimore, MD 21211

Theatrical Rigging Systems, Inc.
P.O. Box 27429
Minneapolis, MN 54427

Tiffin Scenic Studios
136 Riverside Drive
Tiffin, OH 44883

Tobin's Lake Studio
2650 Seven Mile Rd.
South Lyon, MI 48178

Western Service & Supply, Inc.
2100 Stout Street
Denver, CO 80201

2. Rigging and Hardware: Some firms specialize in rigging, curtains, drops, and other special stage hardware.

Peter Albrecht Corp.
325 East Chicago St.
Milwaukee, WI 53202

Becker Studios
2824 W. Taylor St.
Chicago, IL 60612

J.R. Clancy, Inc.
7041 Interstate Island Rd.
Syracuse, NY 13209

Merrill Stage Equipment
6520 Westfall Blvd.
Indianapolis, IN 46220

Levy Hardware Co. Inc.
25 Stuart St.
Boston, MA 02116

3. Curtains and Stage Fabrics

Art Drapery Studios
2756 N. Lincoln Ave.
Chicago, IL 60614

Alan R. Davis Textiles
510 E. 86th St.
New York, NY 10028

Dazian's Inc. (Branches in major U.S. cities)
2014 Commerce St.
Dallas, TX 75201

Knoxville Scenic Studios
P.O. Box 1029
Knoxville, TN 37901

4. Lighting Equipment: Most firms carry a full line of lighting equipment, and some offer rental equipment. Those firms marked with * offer complete consultation and engineering services.

American Stage Lighting
13316 North Ave.
New Rochelle, NY 10804

Berky-Colortron*
1015 Chestnut
Burbank, CA 91502

Capitol Stage Lighting Co., Inc.
475 10th Ave.
New York, NY 10018

Control Devices
785 West 600 North
North Salt Lake City, UT 84054

Decor Electronics Corp.
P.O. Box 606
San Marcos, TX 78666

Electro Controls, Inc.*
2975 South 300 West
Salt Lake City, UT 84115

Electronics Diversified, Inc.
1675 N. W. 216th.
Hillsboro, OR 97123

Grand Stage Lighting
640 W. Lake St.
Chicago, IL 60606

Hub Electric Co.*
171 S. Main St.
Crystal Lake, IL 60014

Kliegl Bros. Lighting*
32-32 48th Ave.
Long Island, NY 11101

Stage Lighting Discount Corp.
346 West 44th Street
New York, NY 10036

Strand-Century, Inc.*
20 Bushes Lane
Elmwood Park, NJ 07407

Strong Electric Co.
522 City Park Ave.
Toledo, OH 43601

Superior Electric Co.*
383 Middle St.
Bristol, CT 06010

Theatre Systems, Inc.
29 School Street
Westfield, MA 01085

Theatre Techniques, Inc.*
60 Connolly Parkway
Hamden, CT 06514

5. Lighting Media: (Plastic & gelatine) See also General Supply Houses.

Barbizon Electric
426 West 55th
New York, NY 10019

Rosco Laboratories
36 Bush Ave.
Port Chester, NY 10573

6. Paint: See also General Supply Houses. (Check local dealers for casein colors.)

Gothic Color
90 Ninth Ave.
New York, NY 10011

Playhouse Colors
771 9th Ave.
New York, NY 10019

Proscenium Products
P.O. Box 252
Andover, NJ 07821

Roscopaint
Rosco Laboratories
36 Bush Ave.
Port Chester, NY 10573

7. Sound Effects Recordings & Tapes: See also General Supply Houses.

Dramatists Play Service
440 Park Ave. South
New York, NY 10016

Thomas J. Valentino, Inc.
150 West 46th St.
New York, NY 10036

Music for the Theatre
425 Central Park West
New York, NY 10025

8. Theatre Sound Systems: Includes companies having intercom as well as full sound systems.

Auditronics, Inc.
3750 Old Getwell Rd.
Memphis, TN 38118

Clear-Com
759 Harrison
San Francisco, CA 94107

Broadcast Electronics, Inc.
4100 North 24th Street
Quincy, IL 62301

Custom Audio Electronics
2828 Stommel Rd.
Ypsilanti, MI 48197

Burke Electronics, Inc.
1703 Jackson
Philadelphia, PA

Terry Hanley Audio Systems, Inc.
329 Elm
Cambridge, MA 02139

David Clark Co. Inc.
370 Franklin St.
Worchester, MA 01604

LANGUAGE ARTS BOOKS

Tandem: Language in Action Series
Point/Counterpoint, *Dufour and Strauss*
Action/Interaction, *Dufour and Strauss*

Business Communication
Business Communication Today!,
 Thomas and Fryar
Successful Business Writing, *Sitzmann*
Successful Business Speaking, *Fryar
 and Thomas*
Successful Interviewing, *Sitzmann and
 Garcia*
Successful Problem Solving, *Fryar and
 Thomas*
Working in Groups, *Ratliffe and Stech*
Effective Group Communication,
 Ratliffe and Stech

Reading
Reading by Doing, *Simmons and Palmer*
Literature Alive, *Gamble and Gamble*
Building Real Life English Skills, *Penn
 and Starkey*
Practical Skills in Reading, *Keech and
 Sanford*
Essential Life Skills Series, *Penn and
 Starkey*

Grammar
Grammar Step-By-Step Vol. 1, *Pratt*
Grammar Step-By-Step Vol. 2, *Pratt*

Speech
Getting Started in Public Speaking,
 Prentice and Payne
Listening by Doing, *Galvin*
Person to Person, *Galvin and Book*
Person to Person, Workbook, *Galvin
 and Book*
Speaking by Doing, *Buys, Sills and Beck*
Self-Awareness, *Ratliffe and Herman*
Literature Alive, *Gamble and Gamble*
Contemporary Speech, *Hopkins and
 Whitaker*
Creative Speaking, *Buys et al.*

Journalism
Journalism Today!, *Ferguson and Patten*

Media
Understanding Mass Media, *Schrank*
The Mass Media Workbook, *Hollister*
Media, Messages & Language, *McLuhan,
 Hutchon and McLuhan*
Understanding the Film, *Johnson and
 Bone*
Photography in Focus, *Jacobs and
 Kokrda*
Televising Your Message, *Mitchell and
 Kirkham*

Theatre
Dynamics of Acting, *Snyder and
 Drumstra*
Play Production Today!, *Beck et al.*
Acting and Directing, *Grandstaff*
An Introduction to Theatre and Drama,
 Cassady and Cassady
The Book of Scenes for Acting Practice,
 Cassady

Mythology
Mythology and You, *Rosenberg and
 Baker*
World Mythology: An Anthology of
Great Myths and Epics, *Rosenberg*

Mystery and Science Fiction
The Detective Story, *Schwartz*
You and Science Fiction, *Hollister*

Writing and Composition
Lively Writing, *Schrank*
Snap, Crackle & Write, *Schrank*
An Anthology for Young Writers,
 Meredith
Writing in Action, *Meredith*
Writing by Doing, *Sohn and Enger*
The Art of Composition, *Meredith*
Look, Think & Write!, *Leavitt and Sohn*
The Book of Forms for Everyday Living,
 Rogers

For further information or a current catalog, write:
National Textbook Company
4255 West Touhy Avenue
Lincolnwood, Illinois 60646-1975 U.S.A.